WALLINGFORD
THE TWENTIETH CENTURY

DAVID BEASLEY

SUTTON PUBLISHING

OXFORDSHIRE BOOKS

Sutton Publishing Limited
Phoenix Mill · Thrupp · Stroud
Gloucestershire · GL5 2BU

First published 2004

 **OXFORDSHIRE BOOKS**

Title page photograph: Station Road,
Wallingford, looking west, *c.* 1907. *(DB)*

British Library Cataloguing in Publication Data
A catalogue record for this book is available from the
British Library.

ISBN 0-7509-3123-X

Typeset in 10.5/13.5 Photina.
Typesetting and origination by
Sutton Publishing Limited.
Printed and bound in England by
J.H. Haynes & Co. Ltd, Sparkford.

*I would like to dedicate this book to my son, Adam,
my daughter, Hayley, and my sister, Wendy.*

Three contestants in the fancy dress competiton held during the peace celebrations in 1919.
Hilda Crook is Peace; on her left is Miss Steel. *(DB)*

CONTENTS

Wallingford Bridge from the air, *c.* 1972. The photograph was taken from a radio-controlled model aircraft. *(DP)*

INTRODUCTION

W hen I was first asked to write this book, I thought that with a collection of over 12,750 images it wouldn't be difficult to compile. The first fifty years were indeed easy to cover, but the second half of the century proved to be a different matter.

Wallingford has changed much over the last hundred years, most of all in the size of its population. In 1900 this stood at 2,700; by 1961 it was almost 5,000; and by the end of the century it had more than doubled again to over 10,000. There were, of course, other changes too: in the years immediately before the First World War the first council houses were built (in St John's Road), the old age pension for men over 70 years old was introduced (in January 1909), the Cottage Hospital was extended and the Cottage Homes were built. The town's two grammar schools were amalgamated in 1904, and six years later a new Boys Council School was opened. Yet the pace of life remained gentle and untroubled.

All this changed, however, with the outbreak of hostilities in August 1914. During four years of war over 2,000 men from Wallingford and the surrounding district served in the forces. Wallingford alone lost eighty men – a high enough figure, but actually an underestimate, because it includes only those resident in the town. If one were to add those born in Wallingford but no longer living there, the number would be considerably higher. Then there were the wounded, estimated at four times the number killed – which would make over 300 casualties from a population of barely 3,000 people. This gives an idea of the sacrifice made by the town. There was sacrifice on the home front, too: with so many away in the forces, the women had to do the work usually done by men, working on the land and in the iron foundries and munitions factories, often for long hours. On top of this they had to look after their children and run a home – a truly magnificent effort.

Between the wars motor traffic began to increase and the narrow streets of Wallingford became congested. Parking seemed to be the biggest problem: there were of course in those early days no official car parks, so people would park anywhere (a trend that seems to be returning today!). Tom Tappin opened his garage in Hart Street in the early 1920s before moving to St John's Road in 1927. In this period there began a move away from working on the land, many going to work at Morris's car factory at Cowley. Wilder's and the Brewery (taken over by Ushers in 1928), both in Goldsmith's Lane, were none the less still the town's biggest employers.

There were other changes, too. A new hospital was built in Reading Road and the old one converted into a new police station. The Regal Cinema first opened its doors in 1934. Clapcot Way council estate was also built in the 1930s. In May 1934

Wallingford celebrated – with some gusto – the Royal Jubilee of George V and Queen Mary, and exactly three years later the Coronation of George VI.

By the late 1930s, however, the storm clouds of war were gathering over Europe. Nationally, the Army, Royal Air Force and Territorial Army (TA) were all being strengthened, as was, at the local level, Wallingford's own TA company. When war at last came in September 1939, Wallingford's Territorials were sent to France. The following year, in the retreat to Dunkirk, the Wallingford boys suffered heavy casualties.

Wallingfordians served in all theatres of the Second World War, some with distinction, including Ernest John Belcher, who was killed on D-Day (6 June 1944) while serving with the Royal Marines, and Captain Wells, who died while courageously attacking a German armoured column with just a revolver.

When the war ended in 1945 there was a massive council house building programme in Wallingford. Sinodun, Andrew and Wilding Roads were built, and the extension of St George's Road and Nicholas Road formed a large council estate. The opening of the Hydraulics Research Station at Howbery Park coincided with the building of the council estate, and some houses were allocated to Hydraulics Research employees who came down from the National Physical Laboratory in London – which caused some ill-feeling in the town. When the atomic research station was opened at Harwell, a further estate was built around Blackstone Road and Norris Drive exclusively for Harwell workers.

The local railway line was closed in 1960. The Association of British Maltsters was built and grew to be a large employer in the town. The Fir estate went up in the 1960s as a mix of both private and council housing. There was a growing need for private housing as people became more affluent, which increased infill-building. All this extra housing, of course, allowed the town's population to rise, so that it now stands (as mentioned above) at over 10,000. But a price was paid. In the 1960s and early 1970s Wallingford lost many of its old buildings, ones that today would probably have been listed. Inevitably, some of the town's character has been destroyed, particularly in the High Street. An archaeological site in St John's Road was another casualty. We have even lost the pinnacles on St Mary's Tower. Let me not give the wrong impression, however. Much of old Wallingford remains; it is just that, with a little more thought, we might have had an even better town to hand on to our children and grandchildren.

Throughout I have tried to make this book as much about the people as the buildings of Wallingford. After all, it is the people who make Wallingford what it is.

David Beasley
2004

Chapter One

1900 to 1910

The Corn Exchange, c. 1909. Built in 1856 by Moses Winter, the Exchange was used for the weekly selling of corn and meat until 1934. Originally designed to be a theatre, it was used in the 1920s and early 1930s as a cinema, until the Regal was opened in St Martin's Street in 1934. The Territorial Army also used it from 1908 to 1925 as their drill hall and armoury; signs to this effect can be seen to the right of the door. In front of the Corn Exchange are various items of farm machinery displayed by Richard Wilder in the hope that farmers attending the market in the Exchange might be tempted to make a purchase. To the right of the Exchange is Thomas Wheeler's grocery shop; Lloyds Bank purchased the premises in March 1914 but did not convert the building to a bank until after the First World War. *(DB)*

In 1901 not only did Wallingford lose its Queen, with the death of Victoria, but it also lost John Kirby Hedges (1811–1901), one of its most prominent citizens. He gave generously to the Grammar School, Cottage Hospital, Almshouses and the Free Library. He had lived most of his life at Wallingford Castle in the house erected by his father some years before. In 1858, at the sale of the Howbery Estates, John Kirby Hedges purchased the grounds and ruins of Wallingford Castle. On 11 April 1901, the day of his funeral, most of the business in town closed at 2 p.m. Large numbers gathered in the market place, while within St Mary's Church final respects were paid by a packed congregation, much of it made up of working-class townsfolk. *(DB)*

Wood Street, 1904, looking south towards St Leonard's Lane. In the background to the right can be seen two men fixing telegraph wires to the pole installed in this year by the National Telephone Company. The young lad with the GPO armband standing to the right of the Corporation dustcart is a telegram boy. The building on the extreme left is St Peter's Rectory; the Revd Samuel Cox was living here at this time. Most of the buildings on the right had all been demolished by the 1930s. The first building on the right was the Particular Baptists (Jireh) Hall, pulled down somewhat later, in the 1950s. Two buildings past the hall stood an iron foundry, which was owned by William Guttridge until his death in April 1886, when the foundry was closed. The premises were then used as a blacksmith's until the building was demolished in 1922, when that area of Wood Street was redeveloped. *(DB)*

Opposite, bottom: The proclamation, 25 January 1901, of the accession of Edward VII, following Queen Victoria's death three days earlier. Within only a few hours of its arrival in the town the proclamation document was being read to a large crowd thronging the Market Place. The Revd A.W. Deacon had informed the various schools of the forthcoming ceremony. Parents, despite the bitterly cold wind, dutifully brought their children. The Mayor (Councillor T. Pettit) read the proclamation, alongside the Town Clerk (Mr Francis Hedges), the Mace Bearer (Mr William Blackwood) and the whole town council (although only a few councillors could actually get on to the balcony). After the reading the crowd, accompanied by a cornet player from the town band, sang the national anthem. *(DB)*

The High Street, Wallingford, *c.* 1904, looking west. Just before the George Hotel is Priscilla and Emily Gardener's confectionery shop, a heaven for small boys. Not being the cleanest of shops, it was not unknown for mice to be seen running around the sweet jars. The man on the left is about to enter Emery's hairdressing saloon; just past him in the white shirt is a butcher outside Leach's shop. In the centre of the picture is a policeman on point duty; there were ten policemen stationed in Wallingford at this time. *(DB)*

Because there was a brewery in Wallingford, there were a large number of public houses: the High Street alone had eleven at one time. In this 1910 picture of Church Lane (formerly French Horn Lane and St Mary's Lane), The French Horn public house can be seen on the left (now 11 Church Lane). Its business must have been small, as there were three other pubs within 100 yards – The Eight Bells was on the corner of Church Lane and St Martin's Street, and The Wagon and Horses stood on the corner of Goldsmith's Lane and the Kine Croft. In the Kine Croft itself was The Coach and Horses. The landlady of The French Horn at this time was Emma Giles, widow of James, who was landlord until his death in 1909. Like many other pubs in the town, The French Horn sold beer only. The pub was finally closed in November 1911, at which time Wallingford had thirteen fully licensed houses, ten beerhouse licenses and four grocer's licenses, giving a total of twenty-seven premises where alcohol could be bought. *(DB)*

Opposite, bottom: St Mary's Street, looking towards the Market Place, *c.* 1908. The police station is on the left. A postman can be seen standing by the main door, delivering mail. Frederick Webb was the inspector in charge at the police station, a position he held until after the First World War. Next door was a cobbler's shop, followed by The Farrier's Arms, where Danny Andrews was the landlord. He later moved to The Greyhound in St John's Road when his pub was closed in 1909. The Farrier's Arms was also known as King William IV and The Railway Arms. The last building on this side was Mrs Emily Briginshaw's shop. Opposite stood The King's Arms; Thomas Lucas was the landlord. It was closed in 1920. Next door was Albert Reynolds' chemist's shop; one door along from that lived Henry Naish. Mr Chapman's shop is on the far right; next to him was Dr Nelson's house. Just past here was the entrance to the six houses of Grainger's Court. *(DB)*

Wallingford Boys' Council School, St John's Road, 1910. The school was for older boys; infants and girls still attended the Kine Croft School. The school was opened in April 1910 by the Mayor (S.L. Hawkins); a few weeks later parents and the general public were allowed in to inspect the school for themselves. The first headmaster was Mr T.H. Astbury (1858–1922), former headmaster of the Boys' National School, Kine Croft. He retired in 1920 because of ill-health. As well as being a teacher he was also a distinguished amateur astronomer, and had the rare privilege of having a star he discovered named after him. *(DB)*

Wallingford Grammar School, *c.* 1906. The building was opened on 10 September 1877 by Edward Wells, MP. It cost £3,000 and had space for 110 scholars. A science laboratory was added in 1898, paid for by John Kirby Hedges. Originally built as two schools, one for boys and the other for girls, the schools were amalgamated in 1904. In 1958 the girls were transferred to Didcot Girls' Grammar School; one of the Grammar's pupils was Ann Packer, who won gold for Britain in the 1964 Olympics. *(DB)*

The woodwork class at Wallingford Grammar School, *c.* 1910. The boys seem rather well dressed for doing woodwork. Few of them would become craftsmen; instead they would join their fathers' businesses or the Army, or perhaps become teachers. *(DB)*

Kine Croft School second-year pupils, *c.* 1903. Back row, left to right: ? Buckingham, ? Nobes, James Shepherd, Stanley Wells, Wilf Thomas, 'Scrog' Wiles, Emma Blissett, Fanny Groves. Third row: Gladys Newin, ? Groves, 'Brock' Cheney, 'Fatty' Gardener, ? Morbey, ? Hatto, Frank Ayres, Wally Frewin. Second row: Jock King, ? Newin, Horace Hatto, Eddie Castle, ? Shepherd, Charles Beasley, Frank Whittick. Front row: ? Wells, ? Hatto, ? Stickley (Heathercroft), ? Groves, George Batten, ? Batten, Bill Blissett, -?-, -?-. *(DB)*

Above: The Wallingford Fair, pictured here in 1904, was very much a family occasion, drawing families from the surrounding villages in large numbers. The sounds of the fair were tremendous: the shouting of the showmen and the stall-keepers, the musical organs, the crack of rifles on the ranges, the banging of drums, the whirl and hum of the many steam engines and the shrill of steam whistles on the roundabouts. Then there were the smells coming from the horses and from oil in the lamps and the steam engines, and the more pleasant aromas of sausages and other meats, of fish being fried and even of rainbow-coloured sweets. All these sounds and smells bombarded your ears and nose the moment you entered the fair. *(DB)*

Below: View of Wallingford Fair, 1904. The boy on the left is a grammar school boy, as can be seen from the portcullis design on his cap. Living in the days when there was no television or radio, children like those in the picture must have really looked forward to the fair, eagerly saving their pennies to spend there. The vans were only allowed to enter the Kine Croft at a set time on the evening before the fair opened. It is hard to imagine now the noise created by the puffing of the traction engines, the clatter of the horses' hooves and the crack of whips as they all passed through the town to the Kine Croft. *(DB)*

Wallingford Michaelmas Hiring Fair, 1890, held annually on 29 and 30 September. These were red-letter days in Wallingford's year. The hiring was done on the first morning and was usually finished by midday. The men who wished to change employment stood in the Market Place, each man wearing a distinguishing emblem in his hat or lapel – the cowman a bunch of cowhair, the carter a length of whipcord or the shepherd a piece of wool. The deal was sealed by the farmer paying a shilling. Once hired, the men wore a ribbon in their hat or lapel. Mr C. Bird's roundabout is being assembled between the obelisk and the Town Hall, a spot it occupied for years until the fair was moved from the town to the Kine Croft. At the time of Mr Bird's death in 1892 he and his wife had had the business for thirty years, and Mrs Bird continued with it for over twenty years more. The life must have been hard, as bad weather would affect both travelling and the takings, but the rewards could be great: during the height of the season the Birds could make as much as £30 a day. This photograph was taken after they had sold their horses (it had taken fourteen to pull all their equipment) and purchased a traction engine. The building behind the roundabout is the Wallingford Bank, managed by Hedges, Wells and Morrell. *(DB)*

Opposite, bottom: The Gay Geraniums, *c.* 1908. The Gay Geraniums performed at many fêtes and regattas in the district, in particular the Goring Regatta, at which they sang each year from 1902 to 1910. They were booked to appear at the Goring Regatta on 29 July 1905, but the weather turned foul. Two weeks later an article written by one of the performers appeared in the *Berks and Oxon Advertiser* describing their journey downriver to Goring. They were towed on a punt by one man, but the wind was so strong that two other men had to be engaged to assist the towing, as there was a real danger of the punt's being swamped. When they finally reached Goring one of their singers fell overboard with their collection box. Fortunately she was rescued, but the money was lost. Despite the weather and no collection box they were able to do their performance and collected 30s. From left to right the performers are: Percy Turner, Eleanor Wilder, -?- and Walter Wilder. The two small boys on the left and right of the picture are Eric and John Turner, Percy Turner's twin sons. *(AW)*

Wallingford Skiff Regatta at Chalmore Reach, 11 August 1906. The weather was hot, and a large crowd gathered in Percy Turner's grounds at Lower Wharf. The photograph shows the finish of the final ladies' doubles race, the Berkshire crew (near the camera) beating the Oxfordshire crew. In the Berkshire crew were Miss Hendley, Miss Deane and Miss E.R. Hendley (cox); in the Oxfordshire crew were Miss D. Curtis, Miss R. Curtis and L.F. Gale (cox). In the evening a large crowd gathered on the lawn – and parties of listeners in boats on the river – at a Café Chantant where the Gay Geraniums performed an excellent programme of popular music. They were encored many times, and among the songs performed were 'The Little Irish Girl' and 'Were I a Mighty Monarch', both sung by Mr Walter Wilder,

and 'The French We Speak at Home', sung by Percy Turner. The enclosure was illuminated with Chinese lanterns. *(DB)*

The Market Place after the blizzard of 26 April 1908, the greatest fall of snow in southern England since the storm of 1881. It was thought that 20 inches of snow fell in 16 hours. Large numbers of trees were damaged owing to the weight of snow on their branches: in Mongewell Park alone, over seventy trees suffered. Mr Harvey du Cros of Howbery Park was motoring down from London when his car became snowbound at the foot of Gangsdown Hill, Huntercombe. The chauffeur struggled on foot to Howbery, a journey of about 4 miles, which took him several hours to complete, but on arrival he found it was impossible to send a horse and trap to rescue Mr du Cros, so he had to spend the night in a nearby cottage. Rail services were also badly disrupted, trains arriving at Cholsey over four hours late; the last train to Wallingford, which should have arrived at 9.15 p.m. on Saturday, did not do so until 2.15 p.m. on Sunday. Most shops in Wallingford had closed by early Saturday afternoon, and the 7 a.m. delivery by the various town carriers on Sunday was delayed until after 3 p.m. (how times have changed!). Sunday dawned warm and sunny, causing the snow to melt very quickly, which in turn caused considerable flooding in the Thames Valley. *(DB)*

The Royal Standard in St Mary's Street, 1901. Ellen Hands (née Neal, of Cholsey) was the landlady from 1890 until 1908, when she married Jimmy Hands, a fellmonger (a man who cures animal skins) from Old Moor Lane (now St John's Road). The Royal Standard was first referred to as a 'beer house' in 1859, when James Cheney was landlord. *(DPY)*

Troops marching over Wallingford Bridge in 1905 on their way to the Hundred Acres field in Newnham Murren as part of army manoeuvres in which nearly 11,000 men were involved. On Sundays visitors were encouraged to visit the camp, where they had an opportunity to hear the various regimental bands. It was estimated that a crowd of some 2,500 (equivalent to the entire population of Wallingford in 1905) visited the camp. These annual camps were a considerable financial boon to local traders and farmers. *(DB)*

Troops at camp in the Hundred Acres field, Newnham Murren, *c.* 1905. Despite the large number of troops in the area, many of whom were allowed into the town, there was little or no drunkenness. *(DB)*

St Alban's Priory, High Street, Wallingford, *c.* 1909. This house, where the Dalzell family lived for a number of years, was demolished in the early 1960s, when Frank Jenkins's garage was built in its place. St Alban's car park was built over what used to be the Priory garden. In view of such change, it is interesting to note the large number of trees to be seen in the picture. *(DB)*

The Alms Houses, Reading Road, Wallingford, *c.* 1904. Behind is the Cottage Hospital, or Morrell's Memorial Hospital, named after Mary Morrell, who was very prominent in raising the money to build the hospital in 1881. With the help of Dr Horn, Miss Morrell rented a cottage in Reading Road and equipped it with three beds. The nursing was at first done solely by Miss Morrell. The Morrell family gave a generous donation to the Cottage Hospital that covered the entire cost of building. The hospital was later converted into the police station, opened on 29 October 1930 by the Mayor (T.E. Wells). As part of the opening ceremony the Mayor, along with the Town Clerk (Major F.R. Hedges), was locked in the cells by the Chief Constable of Berkshire, thus becoming their first occupants. The police station was finally demolished in 1961 to make way for a smaller one. *(DB)*

The Coronation of Edward VII, 9 August 1902. The Coronation had been postponed after Edward suffered an acute attack of appendicitis in June. Although Edward wished the festivities to be carried out as arranged, the regatta organised for 27 June was likewise postponed until the August Coronation. The public dinner was held in the Corn Exchange; for Queen Victoria's golden jubilee in 1887 and diamond jubilee in 1897 the dinner was held in the Market Place. Many of the decorations were not put up until the morning of the celebrations; as a number of ladders can be seen in this picture, it would seem that the photograph was taken that morning. *(DB)*

Wallingford's Church of England Schools, *c.* 1908. This photograph is taken in the playground of the three schools. There was one school each for the boys and the girls, and one for the infants. They were opened in 1861 at the cost of over £2,000 and had a combined capacity of 550 pupils. At the time of this photograph Mr T.H. Astbury was headmaster for the boys, a post he held in all for twenty-eight years, Miss Bessie Woodward Lovejoy was the girls' mistress and Miss Emily Insall was mistress to the infants. A workman at Wallingford Brewery can be seen watching the proceedings from a window opposite the school. *(MG)*

Charles George Crook, fellmonger and wool-stapler of St John's Road, in a Chenard et Walcker touring car, 1902. With him is his daughter, Ada. The photograph is taken in the yard of St John's Farm, St John's Road; the farm was managed by Mr Arthur Holmes. Mr Crook's Fellmonger's Works were in St John's Road opposite what is now Trenchard Close. The car was sold in 1931 for the princely sum of £2. *(JH)*

Wallingford old and new fire engines, June 1903. The picture was taken at the fire station in St Leonard's Square. The engine dated 1836, the old town engine, was pumped by hand; the new 1903 engine was pumped by steam, which provided greater water flow and at higher pressure. This engine was used until 1925, when it was replaced with a Dennis pump. The Fire Brigade gave a demonstration to the Council and the public of the new fire pump's capability in the Kine Croft. *(WM)*

The Free Library in St Leonard's Square, *c.* 1907. The Free Library and Literary Institute were opened in 1871; the library was founded in 1884 but closed down in 1936, unable to complete with the County Library. However, the two stationery shops in Wallingford, Jenkin's and Bradford's, both kept their libraries going until the 1950s. *(DB)*

The roof of the Free Library. After the library was closed the building was used as a Boy Scouts hall and general function hall. Then, at the turn of the nineteenth century, Pettit's used it as a furniture store. A planning application was at one point submitted to turn the library into flats, but thankfully it was purchased by the Methodist Church, who are currently converting it into offices and a function room, so the building will eventually be returned to public use, for which it was originally intended. *(DB)*

Wood Street, *c.* 1906, looking north towards the High Street, on the corner of Hart Street, the turning into which can be seen. Just behind the knife-grinder was the Fat Ox public house; the landlord at this time was Caleb Bosley. The Fat Ox was closed in 1940. Henry Beasley was the last landlord, a veteran of the war in the Sudan, the Boer War and the First World War. He also found time to go gold mining in Canada in 1903 (although unsuccessfully). The houses immediately in front of the grinder were demolished in the early 1960s. There was a passageway passing through one of these houses to a small courtyard – Court 3, Wood Street – which contained three small cottages with a communal yard and washroom. *(DB)*

The cattle market, Wood Street, *c.* 1902. The cattle market was run by auctioneers Franklin and Gale of the Market Place. This site now forms part of the Cattle Market car park. *(DB)*

Pat, granddaughter of Harvey du Cros of Howbery Park, on her favourite pony outside the main door of Howbery Manor House, 1908. Harvey's son, Arthur, was MP for Hastings. In 1913 his house was badly damaged by fire, allegedly an arson attack on the part of the Suffragette Movement. *(DB)*

Gymkhana held in the Wallingford athletic grounds in Reading Road, 1908. The picture shows Miss Collier, nurse to the children of Doctor Walter, when they came second in the decorated mailcart competition. First prize went to Mrs F.K. Weedon and her nurse, Miss Brown, a feat that both ladies repeated the following year. These gymkhanas were usually held on a Wednesday up until 1914; despite the fact that they were held mid-week they were always well attended, on many occasions by over a thousand people. *(DB)*

Station Road, Wallingford, looking west, *c.* 1907. These houses are opposite the old Grammar School. The first two on the left were demolished in the early 1960s. On the far left is Compton's Agricultural Works, from which Compton Terrace got its name, owned by a Mr Baker. *(DB)*

Opposite: Old Rush Court House, *c.* 1907. When Charles Fuller bought Rush Court in 1886 from William Reginald Lybbe Powys-Lybbe he found the old manor house too damp and liable to flooding, so he built a new house on higher ground. This house is now part of the present nursing home. George Denison Faber lived here from 1899, but in 1922 he moved to Howbery Park, where he raised his prize herd of cows. In recognition of his services during the First World War George Faber was given a peerage in June 1918 and took the title of Lord Wittenham. *(CC)*

The pillow-fight on a pole at the 1908 gymkhana. This is probably the final between H.L. Chamberlain and D. Taylor, which Chamberlain won. Apart from the various fancy dress competitions there were a number of novelty races, such as the cigarette and threading-needle race, won by F.J. Gill, the telegram race, won by Miss W. Peck, and a costume race, won by Walter Crook. There was also a whistling race – quite what it entailed is not easy to guess, but it was won by C. Christopher. At nightfall the grounds were illuminated and a dance was held, with music provided by a Hungarian band. *(DB)*

Charles Absolon (1817–1908), arguably Wallingford's finest cricketer. (Those of a different generation, who remember the exploits of 'Flyer' Haycock, may have a different view.) Absolon was born in Wallingford and lived in St Mary's Street. In his mid-twenties he moved to London, where he ran a meat business, but he always finished work by noon so the rest of the day could be spent playing cricket, a game he continued to play into his eighties. He often played with and against W.G. Grace. In a match played at Nunhead in 1873 he bowled to three of England's best batsmen, one of whom was W.G. Grace. He dismissed all three for a total of six runs, W.G. being the highest scorer with four. Like many cricketers of the 1830s and '40s he played in a top hat. He attributed his long life to no drinking and no betting. *(DB)*

Above: Howbery Park Manor House, Crowmarsh Gifford, *c.* 1906. William Seymour Blackstone MP (1809–81) started building a mansion in 1845 but never completed the project, although enough had been built for him to be able to hold a dinner party there for seventy guests. The uncompleted house was sold in 1858 to Count de Mornay, who had it finished by 1860. Henry Bertie Williams-Wynn purchased the house in 1864, living there until his death in 1895. After several attempts at a sale, the house was finally purchased by Harvey du Cros, MP and director of the Dunlop Rubber Company, in 1902. Lord Wittenham (the erstwhile George Faber of Rush Court) bought it in 1922 and used it as a summer residence until his death in 1931. It went on the market again in 1933. Lord Nuffield was interested but thought the reserve price of £9,000 too high. Requisitioned during the Second World War, it was finally purchased by the Government in 1949. The Hydraulics Research Organisation moved on to the site in the summer of 1951. *(DB)*

Lady Wittenham, formerly Hilda Georgina Graham, whose mother was the eldest daughter of the Duke of Somerset. She married George Faber in 1895 and lived with him at Rush Court and later at Howbery Park. This picture was taken on her twenty-first birthday in 1895. *(DB)*

Baden-Powell's Boy Scouts, 8 June 1910. The picture was taken at the opening of the rifle range (next to the Boys' School in St John's Road). The Boy Scouts and members of Wallingford and Crowmarsh Rifle Club line the route to the pavilion. The opening ceremony was performed by Captain J.A. Morrison MP (the tall man with the straw boater), High Steward of Wallingford, who donated the site of the rifle range. In 1911 tennis courts and quoits pitch were also built. The pavilion, which can be seen in the background, was not only used as a rifle range but also as a gymnasium, and in the 1920s and '30s as a dance hall. Also on the site in the 1930s stood a gospel hall. Several times in the 1930s Anglo-Saxon graves were found around the site. Mr Youngman was the first scoutmaster. He later emigrated to Canada and was badly wounded during the First World War while serving with the Canadian Armed Forces. Mr Youngman started Wallingford's Boy Scouts in 1908, but it was not until 1910 that the town formed a Scouts Association to administer them. Trenchard Close was built on this site in the early 1970s. *(JH)*

Lower Wharf, *c.* 1906. Percy Turner is teaching his twin sons, Eric and John, to swim. He ran swimming classes for the public, using this method of tutoring his pupils, which must have been a considerable strain on his arms. Yet it must have been very successful, because in 1905 two of his young pupils, Winnie and Kathleen Peck, swam from Wallingford Bridge to Lower Wharf, a distance of 600 yards; considering the girls were aged only 9 and 10 this was no mean feat. His two boys' portraits were published in the *London Illustrated News* to advertise a patent food; the same advertisements were later to appear in a Chicago newspaper. Percy Turner was well known in Wallingford for his singing of comic songs at various concerts in the town. *(DB)*

Below: Wallingford Post Office, *c.* 1906.
The post office was opened here in June 1893
and closed in 1936. In 1904 there were four
letter deliveries a day, with one on Sundays.
The post office was open from 7 a.m. to 10
p.m. each weekday and for a short time on
Sundays (to sell stamps only); on the floor
above were the telephone and telegraph
rooms. In 1906 the post master was Mr
Collings, who was replaced in 1909 by Mr
Taylor. The mails were brought to the rear of
the premises in Wood Street and taken to the
sorting room on a miniature tramway. In the
1840s just one postman, James Honey, was
able to deliver all the letters in town each day;
by 1900 it took twenty postmen. In 1937
Frank Jenkins converted the building into a
cycle store and later into a garage, which was
closed in the early 1970s. Boots the Chemist
bought the site of the garage and converted it
into one of their stores. *(DB)*

The Cottage Homes, *c.* 1909. The Cottage Homes were opened on 7 April 1900 by Mr T.W. Russell MP, Parliamentary Secretary to the Local Government Board. The homes consisted of three detached blocks, with accommodation for fifteen children and their foster-parents in each; the centre building also had on its top floor some separate accommodation for sick children. The homes were built on workhouse land but were completely separate from the workhouse itself, as it was thought better for the children to be kept away from the workhouse environment. At the same time as the building of the Cottage Homes a new Infirmary for workhouse inmates was also built, with accommodation for forty-six male and thirty female patients. After Mr Russell opened the Cottage Homes (with a silver key), luncheon was served in the Town Hall. *(MG)*

The construction of the Isolation Hospital began in March 1904 after much debate, there being a strong feeling in the town that a brick building was unnecessary: many preferred a transportable iron building that could be moved from place to place as need arose (which had been done in neighbouring towns). It was felt that a hospital (of whatever type) was needed because only a few years earlier there had been an outbreak of typhoid in Cholsey. In Mongewell Churchyard there stands a headstone to three children of the Butler family who all died of scarlet fever within three days of each other. William Daniel Jenkins, editor of the Wallingford paper, the *Berks and Oxon Advertiser*, was one of those against the building, and he refused to publish letters in favour of it. Rowlands Close was later built on the site of the hospital. *(DB)*

On Monday 25 April 1910 the Isolation Hospital in St George's Road was struck by lightning. The damage caused by a single bolt of lightning, which hit the east side of the building, was considerable: one chimney was demolished, a window was blown out, a hole was blown in the wall of the building, the roof on the east side was stripped of all its tiles, and bricks were blown some 120 yards into the surrounding fields. Inside, floorboards from the first-floor landing were driven on-end through the ceiling above and linoleum was driven through the ceiling 10 feet above the floor. The hospital was enveloped in so much smoke that Mr James, living in Blue Mountains (Union Terrace), a couple of hundred yards away, thought the hospital was on fire. Mr George Davis, whose farm adjoined the hospital, was rolling a field some 60 yards away and was also struck by lightning; the two horses pulling the roller bolted. The Matron and several nurses who were in the building at the time were rescued by Mr Davis and Mr James with the aid of a ladder. The Matron and Mr P.C. Slade, a Hospital Board member, can be seen inspecting the damage. *(DB)*

ANOTHER INTERESTING LETTER FROM TROOPER BOSLEY.

Ladysmith Camp.

Dear Father and Mother,—Just a line to say we have relieved Ladysmith at last, and it has been an awful struggle; but it got so hot for them at last they cleared out. Some of the positions they held the the foreign attaches said no human beings could take, but you will have read ere this that we have taken them. We crossed and re-crossed the river again and again, and kept getting to their flanks, and eventually we fairly beat them. In fact the war is nearly over now. If you saw the hills here, you would say it would be impossible to climb such a height, with huge stones to negotiate and trenches to get through. But with all these obstacles their commandos cannot get them to face us. Our chaps have fairly frightened the pluck out of them. Our division alone took 60 prisoners yesterday, and they left a lot of dead and wounded behind. I never had such a job in my life as getting in their wounded. The lyddite makes them as yellow as a canary and the shells inflict ghastly wounds. They left everything behind them again, and as they retreated we could hear the Ladysmith garrison dropping shells into them. They left some of their big guns behind, but they have blown up every railway bridge they came across. They may make another couple of stands, but the Free State men are tired of it and are threatening to shoot Steyn on sight for drawing them into it. They had eaten all the cavalry horses in Ladysmith, and had only a little biscuit left. I had a very narrow escape. I got struck in the chest with a spent bullet. It was not fired at me, for I was quite a mile and a half from the firing line. It went right through a cartridge I had in my bandolier, in which it lodged. I will keep the cartridge to show you. It was a really marvellous escape, and I thanked God very earnestly for the wonderful preservation. I am going to take my boots off to-night. It was so long ago I did so that I really cannot remember when it was. They tell me I look well, and I feel stronger than ever. I shot a pig yesterday, so we are on pork to-day, and we get fowls and lots of other things now and again.

Yours affectionately,
CALE.

This letter was posted from South Africa in April 1900 by Caleb Bosley, son of Caleb and Martha Bosley, the landlord of The Fat Ox public house in Hart Street. Caleb junior was killed in an air raid on London during the Second World War. *(COS)*

LOCAL MEN AT THE FRONT.

Mrs. H. Gibbons, of St. Mary's Street, Wallingford, has received the following interesting letter from her son, Sergt. W. Gibbons, who is serving with General Buller and assisted in the relief of Ladysmith.

Ladysmith Camp, South Africa.

Dear Mother,—I am glad to say I am in the best of health and spirits. I do not think there will be much more fighting, so cheer up. Our Brigade took part in the relief of Ladysmith, and dreadful hard fighting we had before it was relieved. We marched through the streets of Ladysmith, and Sir George White's troops were drawn up on either side of the streets, and cheered us as we passed, and we all cheered Sir George White as we passed him. They were so pleased to see us, and we were pleased, I can tell you, to see them. But they didn't look like soldiers, but more like skeletons. They had been living on horse flesh and one small hard biscuit a-day, and for two months had not had a single pipe of tobacco. The people of the town were leaning up against the walls or sitting down, being too weak to stand. It was a sight I shall never forget, and on their part they will never forget the sight they saw when they saw us in our dirty, ragged kharki with our sunburnt faces. Although we had had nearly three weeks hard fighting we did not feel any the worse for it. They with their clean kharki uniforms, bright buttons and clean faces showed up a bit, but they could see we had some hard times. We had been living on bully beef and hard biscuit, but we knew we could not get anything else under the circumstances. Now we are resting, and getting new kharki and boots, and better food. We stayed on one of the hills we took for two days, and while there lived up to the mark, for the Boers retreated in such a hurry that they left their dinners on the fire, and everything they had behind them—clothing, boots, rugs, blankets, picks, shovels, provisions, also hens and chickens, which we killed and had a good feed. We also found some flour, and remembering that it was Shrove Tuesday, made some pancakes, even on the battlefield. Shells were flying in all directions, but we took no notice of them, as we are so used to them. We also caught a lot of horses.

Your loving son,
W. GIBBONS.

A letter sent from South Africa, April 1900, by William Gibbons to his mother, Mrs H. Gibbons of St Mary's Street. He was serving with General Buller's column, which assisted in the relief of Ladysmith (28 February 1900). *(COS)*

Bridge House, *c.* 1880. This was the home of Colonel Charles Roberts (1845–1916) from 1905 until his death. Cousin to Lord Roberts of Kandahar, he was Colonel of the Argyll and Sutherland Highlanders and later of the Seaforth Highlanders. He served in India, Afghanistan, Burma and Canada, and took part in the famous march from Kabul to Kandahar. In September 1915 he undertook the training of young Army officers in Scotland, but this was to prove too strenuous for him and his health began to fail. Colonel Roberts returned to his home in Wallingford to recover. A journey to Oxford and back in an open car proved to be the last straw: he suffered a heart attack, from which he died in April 1916. *(DB)*

The December 1910 general election crowds outside Dyer's upholsterer's in the Market Place. At a meeting in the Corn Exchange Lord Dundonald spoke in support of Major H. Henderson, the Conservative candidate. In his speech there was some disagreement with the author Jerome K. Jerome over the price of meat in Germany. Mr Jerome priced German meat at 3*s* a pound, whereas Lord Dundonald said it was only 1*s* 8*d* a pound. With customary wit, Mr Jerome concluded the argument by saying that Lord Dundonald was probably referring to horse meat. *(DB)*

The Conservative 'Battle Wagon' for the December 1910 general election (the second of that year), outside the Green Tree in St Leonard's Square. The man nearest the cart is Alfred Giles, landlord of The Green Tree. The Conservative candidate was Major H. Henderson, a Boer War veteran; he won in December, as he had in the February election, beating the Liberal candidate in each case. *(KC)*

The greenhouse in the Castle Grounds, *c*. 1906. The greenhouse backed on to the wall of St Nicholas's College, which stood within the Castle grounds. The oldest man in the picture is Frederick James Wells, who worked at the Castle for forty-six years.

Below: The Hedges family's Landau, standing outside the front door of Castle House, *c*. 1906. The coachman is Benjamin Coles, who was also coachman to local philanthropist John Kirby Hedges.

A view of St Nicholas's College in the Castle Grounds, *c.* 1906. In the 1930s and '40s the building on the right was the home of a small private museum belonging to the Hedges family. *(DB)*

The top of the mound looking east towards St Nicholas's College, *c.* 1906. Castle House would have been on the left. On the back of this postcard, Rosemary King (formerly Miss Hedges) wrote: 'This is the house that was', as she was born in Castle House and lived here until she was married in 1937. She witnessed the demolition of the house in 1972. *(DB)*

Chapter Two

1911 to 1920

The proclamation of the accession of George V, Monday 9 May 1910. (King George had acceded to the throne three days before.) The Mayor, Sidney Hawkins, is reading the proclamation from the Town Hall balcony to a crowded Market Place. Accompanying him are Aldermen B.W. Hilliard, Thomas Pettit and Henry Wells, Councillors S. Naish and J. Wilder, the Canon Deacon, the Town Clerk, Francis Hedges, and Sergeant-at-Mace Mr G. Cheney. The local Territorials, under Sergeant E.O. Payne, provided a Guard of Honour; the Boy Scouts were also represented. *(DB)*

The Town Hall on the Coronation of George V, 22 June 1911. The wind was quite strong all day, but it helped to keep most of the rain away. The town was very highly decorated by Councillor S. Naish, as can be seen in this photograph. He used 200yd (183m) of cloth and over a thousand lights. Mr H. Naish of St Mary's Street displayed a silk flag that was first flown for Queen Victoria's Coronation on 28 June 1838. The photograph shows the start of the United Service, the clergy and ministers conducting it from the balcony of the Town Hall. The umbrellas are being used not as protection from the sun but to keep the light rain off. The dinner (served at 1 p.m.), to which only males over fourteen years were invited, was held in the Kine Croft and served in four marquees. At 3.30 p.m. the ladies (320) and infants (97) were served tea in three tents, two of which had six tables each, while the third, smaller, tent had just two. Mrs Lloyd of the Market Place provided the tea. For the children aged between five and fourteen tea was served at 5 p.m. Some 456 children took part, gathering in one or other of two tents – one for girls and one for boys. While the children were having their tea the Mayor (Mr Sidney Hawkins) presented them with their Coronation mugs. *(DB)*

The High Street looking east, with the Lamb Hotel on the left, on George V's Coronation Day, 22 June 1911. The high winds that plagued the day can be seen clearly from the flapping flags. Along with the George Hotel, Walter Hunt's shop (centre of picture) was commended by the *Berks and Oxon Advertiser* for the excellence of its decorations. Although the Japanese lanterns and fairy lights were badly damaged by the high winds, the effect at night was still very striking. *(COS)*

Arthur Cleaver's grocer's and butcher's shop in Wood Street, *c.* 1912. In 1910 Wallingford had a population of 2,700, around one-quarter of today's. There were seven butchers, nine grocers, three bakers, twenty-four hotels and public houses, and a permanent police force of ten officers. Today there are just eight hotels and public houses, and one baker. *(COS)*

John Tombs ironmonger's in the Market Place, *c.* 1912. Tombs bought out James Preston's ironmongery in about 1900, later extending his shop by buying out Henry Dyer's upholstery business in 1912. He continued to run the business until his death in 1920. Frank Whiteman became manager in 1920, and took over the business in 1922, changing the name to Whiteman's. Whiteman's closed in the 1960s and today the premises is owned by Lloyd's chemists. *(ML)*

The London Meat Company's butcher's shop on the corner of Wood Street and the High Street, *c.* 1910. Previously the premises was occupied by Edwin Fastnedge, a dairyman. The shop next door was a tobacconist's and hairdresser's run by Walter Emery; it remained a hairdresser's for ninety years. Leonard Shepherd, the grocer, took over the shop in 1935 when Walter Emery died. *(DB)*

Madeline Harvey dressed as Grace Darling, a costume she wore to a fancy dress party held in connection with the Young Helpers' League at the Town Hall on 3 January 1912. In the under-8s class first prize went to Marjorie Hawkins, dressed as a Japanese girl; Kathleen Hinton won second prize as Cupid. In the over-8s class first prize was won by Betty Freeman, dressed as Summer; in second place was Isabel Henson. Madeline Harvey lived at 2 High Street with her parents, Thomas and Alice. Thomas worked as a tailor. *(Unknown)*

Cooks of the Royal Engineers in camp at Bow Bridge, June 1914. For three weeks in June the 2nd Division Royal Engineers were camped at Bow bridge, near Wallingford. At the end of the three weeks they were replaced by the 1st Division. The training consisted of building pontoon bridges across the Thames. During this training civilians were encouraged to come and watch the construction. The building of these bridges was shot by the Army Film Unit for training purposes, but the film was also shown to the public in cinemas around the country. *(DB)*

Summer 1914. During the time the 1st Division were at camp a sports day was held. Most of the events were of a military nature, but the pontoon race was open to civilian crews of ten from Wallingford and District. Wallingford, Cholsey and Brightwell each entered crews. All had difficulty in adapting to this unusual craft, but Wallingford won the event mainly because of their superior steering: the other crews fouled the river bank as they neared the winning post. In the Wallingford crew were H. Walters, B. Clinch, W.D. Jenkins (junior), H. Harris, H. Tustain, F.A. Snow, J.H. Hollowell, P.J. Lloyd, J. Hoult, Messrs. James and Howard. (DB)

The longest boat on the River Thames – a 197ft rowing boat. It was made by the Royal Engineers in 1914 from wood and canvas but could only be rowed in one direction. The crew would have to turn it around for the return journey. (DB)

Crane & Shepherd's grocer's shop, in the High Street, *c.* 1916. The building was formerly Overthorpe House, and was sold in March 1914 to a Mr Hurst of Oxford, who had the house converted into a shop, which he leased to Crane and Shepherd in the same year. When Charles Crane died in 1942 the name was changed to Shepherd's, which Leonard Shepherd (a former Mayor of Wallingford) continued to manage until his death in 1953. His son Arthur ran the business until he died in 1964, when the shop was converted into a laundrette and is now the Laundry Express. In January 1933 Leonard was going to a fancy dress dance dressed as a tramp: on his way to the dance he decided to call into his shop, and as he was unlocking the front door he was arrested by the police, who thought he was a vagrant. *(DB)*

The High Street, *c.* 1918. The toyshop on the left is George Relf's. As well as a toyshop it was also the registry office for servants. The postcard that this picture was taken from was sold here. Two shops up from Relf's was John Tomb's Temperance Hotel; next to that was Emery's tobacconist's, and opposite stood Gardener's sweetshop. The International Store can be seen on the right. Next door is Thomas Gibbon's Bakery, opened in 1870. In 1936 one of the Gibbons family was made Captain of the *Queen Mary*, only to have his posting cancelled within a few months on the grounds that the liner had no need of two captains. *(DB)*

John Tomb's Temperance Hotel, *c.* 1914. Despite the presence of a brewery in the town, there was a strong temperance movement in Wallingford. A Temperance Hall stood in St Mary's Street, and there was often a temperance tent at Wallingford Fair. *(DB)*

The 104th Oxfordshire Agricultural Society Show, Station Road, Wallingford, 20–22 May 1914. The show was held in Mr Steel's field, near the railway station. Over 9,000 people visited the show over two days; it was thought to be one of the best in the Society's history. Special goods trains were arranged to carry the exhibits to Wallingford (over 550 were required). To entertain the visitors who stayed overnight the 4th Dragoon Guards, who played throughout the day at the show, gave a concert in the Corn Exchange, which was full to capacity. The Society President, Mr G.D. Faber of Rush Court, visited the show on the first day. Cattle, horses, sheep and pigs were shown, and there were eighty-four stands of farm implements, in which Richard Wilder's were very prominent. *(DB)*

Wallingford ladies making a street collection in June 1917 for war wounded, each lady representing a month of the year; October was Hilda Cook. *(OR)*

Wednesday 5 August 1914: the Wallingford Territorials, C Company, 4th Royal Berkshire Regiment, leaving for Reading. The Territorials had mustered a total of fifty-four men on the Tuesday evening at their headquarters in the Corn Exchange, where they stayed overnight. At midday, in a heavy thunderstorm, they headed for the railway station. Proceeding them was the Boy Scout Bugle Band, and over a thousand townsfolk followed them to the station. The engine was decorated with Union Jacks, and the train moved off to the loud cheering of the crowds and the sound of detonators on the line. After a short stay at Cosham, near Portsmouth, the battalion moved to Swindon on the Sunday night. Here on the following Tuesday the battalion was asked if it would volunteer for foreign service. They were given 10 minutes to consider; the majority volunteered. *(DB)*

The Market Place, *c.* 1916. The lorry parked in front of the Town Hall has the remains of an aircraft on its trailer. During the First World War a number of aircraft crashed around Wallingford. Could this be the aeroplane that crashed in 1916 in the fields between Wallingford and Cholsey? The pilot, Esmond O'Hanlan, stayed the night with the Revd Mr Raynor, much to the consternation of the special police force. *(WM)*

Ladies working at Walter Wilder's Foundry, Crowmarsh, *c.* 1917. With most men serving in the forces, women had to take over their jobs. Appeals were often made on behalf of Wilder's to the Wallingford Tribunals against their staff being called up, but only with mixed success. Most times the call-up was deferred for just a few months, to give Wilder's time to find a female replacement. Some of those replacements can be seen in this picture. The War Tribunals Boards, consisting of a number of local people plus a military representative, were where appeals against call-up could be heard. Appeals could be made on grounds of domestic hardship, working in a reserved occupation or being a conscientious objector. *(AW)*

Top: The 1st Wallingford Volunteer Battalion, Royal Berkshire Regiment, 1918. The photograph was taken in the Paddock sports ground, Reading Road. The battalion was made of men unfit or too old for service in France. Francis R. Hedges is the man seated in the front row with the walrus moustache. *(WM)*

Above, left: Corporal Leonard Gale, the Queen's Own Oxfordshire Hussars (killed 26 May 1915). The second son of J.J. Gale, he was thirty years old when he died. A very keen cricketer, footballer and rower, he was a partner in the auctioneers Franklin and Gale of the Market Place. *(DB)*

Above, left: Second Lieutenant Douglas Gale, elder brother of Leonard (wounded in France, 1916). Douglas Gale was later made Commanding Officer of the 4th Battalion, B Company (Territorials), Royal Berkshire Regiment. He went to France again in January 1940 but was sent home just before the German attack because he was considered by then to be too old for active service. *(COS)*

Thomas George Tickner, only son of Thomas and Jane Tickner of 17 Market Place, Wallingford. Thomas was an old Wallingford County Grammar School boy, and a fine local sportsman. Before the First World War he worked as a clerk for Walter Wilder & Sons at the Crowmarsh ironworks. In 1908 he joined the Territorials, in which he achieved the rank of sergeant. He joined the Royal Berkshire Regiment in August 194, and, after serving some time in camp at Chelmsford (it was from here that this postcard was sent) he went to France. Within a few days of arriving he was transferred to the South Lancashire Regiment, with the rank of lieutenant. On 1 September 1916 he died from wounds received three days earlier. *(CG)*

Below: Thomas George Tickner's headstone at Puchevillers British Cemetery, the Somme. This cemetery contains the graves of men who died at Casualty Clearing Stations 3 and 44 in 1916. It was to Casualty Clearing Station 3, that Tickner was taken on 29 August 1916, after being wounded by machine-gun fire in an attack on the Hindenburg Trench. *(DB)*

Above: German prisoners of war helping with the harvest at Hithercroft, *c.* 1918. German prisoners of war arrived in Berkshire from as early as 1914, when part of Newbury race course was used as a PoW camp. *(JB)*

Mr Thomas Harvey in the uniform of Wallingford Town Band. Mr Harvey was a tailor and lived at 2 High Street; he was the father of Madeline Harvey. Wallingford had a long tradition of brass bands, the oldest possibly being the Welcome Brass Band, named after the temperance coffee house of the same name in St Leonard's Lane. The fact that the band was linked with the temperance movement caused a stir, and a number of letters were written to the *Wallingford Times* in January 1886 pointing out that when the band played in the streets at Christmas time, players eagerly consumed the beer purchased for them by a grateful public. *(Unknown)*

May 25/15,

My dear Mother and Father —Am just out of the trenches. We went in last night at 12 p.m. to make an attack. The 8th were the attacking party. We were taken up to the first line trench and my platoon had to go out in front and place 12 bridges over a ditch and then come back and take up ammunition after the attack was made. We got the bridges out all right and got back, but had two men killed doing it. Then our Major told me off to stay with him, but I was no butt man and when the attack commenced I beat it out and over the parapet along with the boys. Our Major did not go out at all, so am glad I didn't stay with him. It was nearly light 3,30 a.m, but the boys went across that 200 yards like mad men yelling all the time. We got across the brook and lay down to get our breath and then we all got up again and made the final rush. We formed a fine line and that proved too much for the Germans who beat it out and back into the next trench; we all filed in and had taken the position. We held it all day and none of us had a thing to eat, and at 1,30 a.m, were relieved and right glad we were too. We expected them to make a counter attack but they were too scared. We lost a lot of men in the attack and with shell fire. Our Company lost 60 men and 2 officers. The battalion has only 6 officers left and lost 250 men yesterday. It is awful, but it is our duty. Some men lose their nerves. but it can't be helped, it is an awful sight to see the boys pop over and to see some of the sights their shells make of a man. However the Lord was good to me and to Latter too, for we both got across safely and got out safely and are both here now. Will you take this down to Mrs. Latter ? Ern asked me to tell you just to let his people know that he is all right. He would have written but is too busy now dotting out the casualty list. He will write to-morrow. I think they will have to take us back again for another rest. Brought the men in to-night but the boys can't walk far, they are too tired and cut up. Ern and I got on fine, neither of us got a scratch. Will write later. We did the trick and took the trench. Love to all,

TOM

Best regards to Mr. and Mrs. and Kaile Latter.

A letter from Flanders, dated 25 May 1915, from Thomas Jenkins, who served with the Canadians. Thomas was the son of Daniel Jenkins, the publisher of the *Berks and Oxon Advertiser*. The 'Ern' mentioned in the letter is Ernest Latter, the son of James Alfred Latter, who served from 1914 to 1918 with the 5th Battalion Canadian Infantry (Saskatchewan Regiment). He was awarded the Military Cross and by the end of the war had been promoted to captain. Having survived all the horrors of the war, Ernest unfortunately died of influenza in December 1918. He had just been offered the post of Chief of Police in Yorkton, Canada, and was to have been married on his next leave to Miss Beisley, daughter of the High Street jeweller. *(COS)*

Francis R. Hedges, 1917, with his daughter, Rosemary Jennifer (1914–74), and his son, John Francis (1917–83). Rosemary Hedges married twice – once in 1937 to Captain Wells, and for the second time to Brigadier Horace King in 1951. She was awarded the OBE in 1951 and was a Lieutenant-Colonel in the Women's Royal Army Corps (WRAC). John Hedges was knighted in 1958 and was awarded the Freedom of the Borough in November 1971. *(DB)*

Below: Alfred Perry, of St John's Road, Wallingford, aged one year, winning first prize in the Peace Celebrations, July 1919. The celebrations were held in very wet weather. It was so bad that the open-air dancing which was to be held in the Bull Croft was postponed until the following Wednesday. The programme of celebrations started with sports in the Bull Croft. The 1- and 2-mile bicycle races caused the most interest, Arthur Honeybone's twin sons taking the honours in each race. *(DB)*

The Peace Celebrations in the Market Place, Wallingford, July 1919. It was a strange coincidence that heavy rain fell during these celebrations, as it also rained heavily when the Territorials left Wallingford for France in August 1914. *(DB)*

The invitation to the dinner given to all returning servicemen in 1919. In November 1919 the inhabitants of Wallingford gave a dinner in the Corn Exchange and the Town Hall for all servicemen who had served in the First World War. Over 350 servicemen attended. Mr R. Bosley of The Cross Keys was the caterer, and Messrs Chamberlain and Sons of St Leonard's Square prepared the meal. After the meal the Mayor (Charles Rogerson) gave a short speech in which he mentioned that Wallingford men had won fifteen medals during the war. *(MM)*

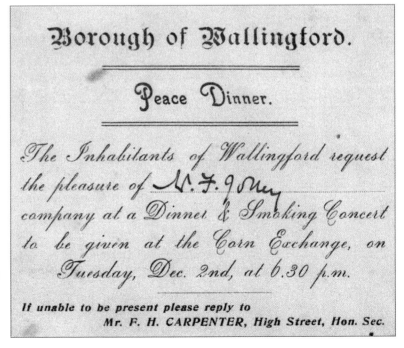

Borough of Wallingford.

Peace Dinner.

The Inhabitants of Wallingford request the pleasure of Mr. F. J. Ory *company at a Dinner & Smoking Concert to be given at the Corn Exchange, on* Tuesday, Dec. 2nd, at 6.30 p.m.

If unable to be present please reply to
Mr. F. H. CARPENTER, High Street, Hon. Sec.

Charles Sadler, who served with the Horse Artillery during the First World War. His daughter, Ivy, remembers (although she was only two at the time) that when her father left for India in 1915 she was frightened by the sound of his spurs. He was a very good sportsman, playing football for teams in Reading and winning several prizes for running. *(IA)*

Phillip's timber yard at the Upper Wharf, Wallingford, *c.* 1920. George Phillips occupied this site between 1919 and 1938. Its location on the banks of the river was chosen because much timber was moved around the country by barge at this time, but as road and rail services improved, and the canal system went into decline, the yard closed. *(RL)*

Chapter Three

1921 to 1930

The war memorial was unveiled on 22 May 1921 by the Lord Lieutenant of Berkshire
(Mr J.H. Benyon). The memorial was designed by Mr Guy Dawber and consists of a
bronze statue of Peace. The statue and the bronze panels were by Mr George
Alexander of Chelsea. The memorial is made of Portland stone and was built by
Honeybone's of Wallingford. *(DB)*

The unveiling of the war memorial, 22 May 1921. The children of those killed during the war are laying down bunches of wild flowers gathered from the fields and woods around Wallingford, each in turn searching the panels for their fathers' names. Mr Rogerson, the Mayor of Wallingford, was the first to lay a wreath, followed by many others, but the most poignant sight was that of the children with their bunches of flowers. *(COS)*

Right: The Stickley Memorial. This memorial used to hang in the hall of the Cottage Homes in memory of a former inmate, Frederick Morris Stickley, who died of pneumonia at the end of the First World War. He was admitted to the Cottage Homes in April 1900, making him one of its earliest occupants. He left in June 1904 to join the Royal Navy and at the outbreak of war in 1914 he volunteered for submarine duty, in which he served until his death at Haslar in November 1918. *(TJ)*

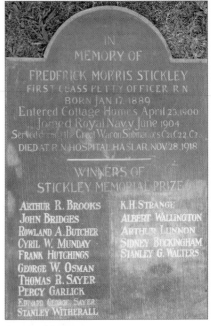

Below: The north end of Wood Street, c. 1920. The first two houses, which form a slight curve to the left of the centre, were so badly damaged in a gas explosion in March 1937 that they had to be demolished. Mr Aubrey Cross, a dairyman, had a milk bottle washing plant next to the demolished houses from the late 1920s until well into the 1950s. The row of terraced houses on the corner of St Peter's Street and Wood Street were demolished in about 1962. Fred Atkins, a chimney sweep, lived at no. 2 in this terrace. He was the father of George Atkins, the manager of the Regal Cinema. *(DB)*

Above: The Toll House at Wallingford Bridge, 1927.
The Toll House was built in 1819, but tolls ceased
being collected in May 1881; from then until 1934
the house was a private residence. At the time of this
photograph Mr H. Batten lived there. The Toll House
was finally pulled down in 1935, despite considerable
opposition in the town. Berkshire and Oxfordshire
County Councils, however, considered the cost of
repair (£250) too much. Stone seats were erected in
its place. It is interesting to note that the photographer
could park his car on the bridge without causing a
traffic jam – an indication of the scant amount of
traffic passing through Wallingford in 1927. *(COS)*

St Mary's Street, *c.* 1928. Champions is on the right,
where the stepladder is hanging. Next door is The
White Hart public house (the landlord was
Mr Cheney), followed by Millward's shoeshop and
Jenkin's printing works, where the *Berks and Oxon
Advertiser* was printed until 1942, when it closed
because of paper shortages during the war. It didn't
reopen until 1949, but then it was printed in
Watlington. The Dolphin public house follows, and
the Cash Draper Store is the last in the row. *(DB)*

Wallingford Brewery staff at the time of Ushers take-over, 1928. The photograph is taken in the brewery yard, now the car park for the Masonic Hall. Wallingford Brewery, in Goldsmith's Lane, belonged to the Wells family from 1720 until Usher took it over in 1928. It was not the only brewery in the town: Hilliard's had one as well, at the opposite end of Goldsmith's Lane. The buildings were converted into dwellings in the 1980s. *(HW)*

Mr H. Waite turning the seed corn in the drying-room at Hunt's Mill House, Goldsmith's Lane, *c.* 1931. The mill, built in 1930, was very up to date for its time. All the machinery was power-driven, and it was used for cleaning and dressing seed corn and for compounding animal feed. *(DB)*

The River Thames in flood at Preston Crowmarsh, 1927. The difficulty with generating electricity during flooding can be seen in this picture. Despite the floods, staff are bringing petrol to run the tank engine. The building in the background is The Swan Inn. The Wallingford and District Electric Supply Company was taken over by the Wessex Electricity Company in about 1936. *(TD)*

Preston Crowmarsh Mills, 1927. The mill (once the property of Lord Wittenham) was used to generate electricity for Wallingford, Benson and Crowmarsh from Wallingford Bridge as far as the Bell public house. The Wallingford and District Electric Supply Company was formed in 1923. Messrs Edmundsons were hired to oversee the installation and running of the plant. The cost of the installation was £12,000, £7,000 of which was raised locally by selling shares for *2s 6d* each; the remaining £5,000 was met by Edmundsons. Electricity was first generated in 1924 by using the two waterwheels, supplemented with a tank engine during periods of high demand and when flooding made it impossible to use the wheels. The offices for the Wallingford and District Electric Supply Company were at 62 High Street. *(DB)*

Chamberlain's staff outing, 1928. Thomas Chamberlain had a grocer's shop on the south side of St Leonard's Square which he purchased from George Gibbons in 1903. It was here that loaves of bread could be bought still warm from the oven, and Jack Page would grind your coffee while you waited. The business down in 1963. *(COS)*

The opening of the Cottage Hospital, 17 July 1929. The Cottage Hospital replaced the old Morrell Memorial Hospital, which was opened in 1881. The old hospital was converted into a police station and was used as such until *c.* 1960. The Cottage Hospital was built by Bosher's of Cholsey and cost £13,500, of which £10,000 was raised by donations. The picture shows (left to right): Mrs Herbert Morrell; Sir John Wormald of the Springs, North Stoke; behind him, the Revd A.H. Caldicott; Miss Laws, the Matron; the Mayor, Mr T.E. Wells; and the Town Clerk, Frances Hedges. The world-famous contralto Dame Clara Butt sang the hymn 'Now thank we all our God', followed by the national anthem. *(JA)*

Opposite, bottom: The Girls' Grammar School in the early stages of a paper chase, *c.* 1930. Considering the cross-country was probably at least 2 or 3 miles long, the girls seem a little overdressed. The shop doorway with the columns either side is Walter Hunt's corn merchant's shop. *(JD)*

Dame Clara Butt (1872–1936) and her husband, Robert Kennerley Rumford, a well-known baritone, at the opening of the Cottage Hospital, 17 July 1929. Dame Clara lived at Prospect House, North Stoke, Oxfordshire. She, her husband and her three children are all buried in the churchyard there; the lych gate is dedicated to her son, Roy, who died in 1923. Whenever available she willingly participated in local events, at which she would inevitably sing. She started the Women's Institute at North Stoke and was its first president. When Germany signed the Peace Treaty of Versailles in 1919 the cricket match between North Stoke and Ipsden was stopped for a short time while she sang the national anthem. She once asked friends from the world of opera to come to North Stoke, and they gave a concert in the village hall. Her ghost is said to haunt one of the rooms at the Springs Hotel at North Stoke. (JA)

Wallingford fire station, 1929. The fire station was moved from New Road to Station Road when a new station house was built in 1924 at a cost of precisely £2,022. It was officially opened on Wednesday 1 July 1925 by the Mayoress, Mrs Richard Wilder. Not only was a new fire station provided, there was also a new Dennis motor pump (fire engine), and new ladders and a hose. The first occupants of the flat that used to be above the fire station were William Moore and his family. Some of the firemen in the 1920s and '30s included Charles Peedle (Station Officer), Bill Field, Bill Herman, Pat Harvey, Harry Quainton, Alec Honeybone, Rufus Green Freddie King, and Len Jones (landlord of the Greyhound public house). *(JA)*

An advertisement for a British Legion fête held in the Bull Croft, 1928. A very large number of people attended this fête. The Great Western Railway laid on special trains from Cholsey, and motor coaches came from as far afield as Reading. The King's Dragoon Guards gave a demonstration of tent-pegging. Unfortunately, at a certain point one of the Dragoons' horses bolted and threw its rider; he was treated for a broken collarbone where he fell in the ring by Dr E.C. Walter. The winners of the lucky programme were Charlie Wadley of Forest Row and Frank Woodley of Crowmarsh, Hilda Shepherd winning the junior prize. *(DB)*

MONSTER FETE

arranged by the

WALLINGFORD BRITISH LEGION

IN THE BULL CROFT, WALLINGFORD

ON SATURDAY, JULY 21st,

BAND OF KING'S DRAGOON GUARDS

MUSICAL RIDE BY THE KING'S DRAGOON GUARDS

FULL DRESS UNIFORM (PRE-WAR)

also

TENT-PEGGING DISPLAY

MOTOR CYCLE GYMKHANA

GRAND DISPLAY OF FIREWORKS.

Full Particulars on Posters and Handbills.

SPECIAL LATE TRAIN LEAVES WALLINGFORD at 11.15 p.m. Stopping at all Stations to READING & DIDCOT.

H. F. WITHRINGTON,

Hon. Organising Secretary.

Three friends, *c.* 1928. From left to right: *?* Westbrook, Thomas Charles Wright, a torpedo officer serving on HMS *Hood,* and Bill Tappin. Wright was killed when the *Hood* was sunk by the *Bismarck* in 1941. Bill Tappin owned and managed Tappin's Coaches until the 1990s. *(BT)*

The Anglo-American Oil Company Fordson lorry, *c.* 1928. It is parked in Wood Street, outside the old post office stables. This building was knocked down to make way for part of the Cattle Market car park, the entrance to which was to be just behind the lorry. *(DB)*

Aerial view of Castle House and the Bull Croft, *c.* 1920. Castle House, on the left of the picture, sits atop Castle Banks; at this time it was the home of the Hedges family. In the 1950s it became an old people's home but was pulled down in 1972, which caused considerable uproar in the town. Castle Street is the row of houses running across the picture. At the bottom of the picture, just above paths in the Bull Croft, can be seen Croft House, with two trees growing on its lawn. *(DB)*

St Anthony's School, *c.* 1928. This was a private preparatory school in the High Street run by Miss Violet Hedges. The children had the run of the Castle Grounds, as can be seen. Many local children from the middle and upper classes attended the school, its most famous pupil being the actress Dulcie Grey. The school closed in the early 1940s. *(MV)*

The boys' dormitory at St Anthony's School, *c.* 1935. It is interesting to see that each bed has a teddy bear lying on it. *(JJ)*

No. 41 High Street, *c.* 1924. This house and three others were situated opposite today's fish and chip shop. The people in the picture are (left to right) Alfred Alder, his mother Lucy Alder and William (Bill) Alder, his brother. Alfred married Hilda Shepherd, the daughter of Leonard Shepherd, ex-Mayor of Wallingford, in the 1930s. These houses were demolished in another act of developer vandalism in the 1960s. *(Mr Alder)*

The Lamb crossroads, *c.* 1922. Walter Hunt's, the corn and seed merchants, took over the house on the corner that belonged to Mr P.E. Long and converted it into a shop in 1923. The shop next door (no. 62) belonged to George Butcher, a boot and shoe dealer, and at no. 60 was William Moss, a tailor. *(WM)*

Opposite: A party of local farmers who went on an eight-day trip to Denmark, in March 1930, to inspect the agricultural systems in use there. They visited a number of farms and were impressed by the co-operative system of farming used in Denmark so much, that when they returned they held a meeting in the Town Hall to discuss the possibility of starting a co-operative creamery which was built and started in Wallingford in 1931. The farmers in the picture are, left to right, Mr H. Hansen, son of Mr A.T. Hansen of Blackall's Farm, Cholsey; Andrew Hedges of Foulscote, near Wallingford; Walter C. Hunt of South Moreton; Mr A.T. Carr of Turner's Court; Frank Young of Newnham Murren, Wallingford; Vernon Drewitt of Slade End, Wallingford; and Frank Stevenson of Hithercroft, Wallingford. While in Denmark they visited the parents of Mr J.M. Thielman, who worked as foreman on Mr C.L. Hansen's farm until in 1929 he was accidentally shot with his own shotgun. *(TM)*

The Wallingford area often suffers from high winds. In 1932 a mini-hurricane whirled along Howbery Park. It travelled down the park's main drive, breaking branches off elm trees before uprooting one and sending it crashing into the lodge house at the main gate. *(DB)*

Wallingford Carnival, Wednesday 9 July 1930. The parade is passing down St Martin's Street. This part of the parade is the decorated cycles and prams. The winner of the decorated cycles was Stanley Evans, second came Sybil Johnson and third was Michael Latter. The winner of the decorated prams was Mrs Absolom, Mrs M.L. Whiteley coming second. After the parade there was a sports meeting in the Bull Croft, a pony gymkhana, a tennis tournament, a lovely-ankle contest (won by Miss Painter), a dance display and, finally, in the evening a carnival dance in the Pavilion in St John's Road. *(DB)*

Wallingford Carnival, 1930. The pirates at the carnival with their collection boxes, with which they used to 'rob' spectators in order to raise money for the Cottage Hospital. *(DB)*

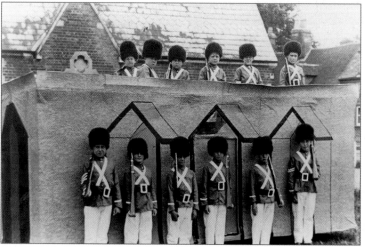

The schoolchildren's float at the 1930 Carnival – an old castle, with living 'toy' soldiers. Pettit's the drapers were the winners of the Class 1 and the Class 2 competition. Among the winners in the sports were (80yd race, boys) Alf Perry, (100yd race, boys) P. Strange, and (80yd race, girls) R. Walters, Joan Messenger coming second. *(DB)*

Chapter Four

1931 to 1940

A 'stop-me-and-buy-one' ice-cream bicycle, Mackney, *c.* 1931. The boy on the bicycle
is Charles Rickards, who lived at Mackney Farm, Brightwell. *(CR)*

Egerton Road, 1930, looking towards Croft Road. The little girl playing is Connie Leaver, who later married Frank Green. The houses in the far distance were knocked down just before the Second World War. During the war an air raid shelter was built on the waste ground. Connie's father worked for the post office for forty-five years. During the First World War he saw active service in the Middle East and France. When his Regiment was returning home in 1917, the ship was torpedoed and quickly sank. After spending some time in the water, Mr Leaver was able to scramble aboard an empty canvas boat that drifted by. During the night he was able to pick up a number of servicemen. The next day they were picked up by a British gunboat. *(MG)*

Below: Mrs Colquhoun with her twin boys Tony and Claude and her daughter in the front garden of the Grammar School. Mrs Colquhoun's husband, was a master at the Grammar School for many years. *(JD)*

Tom Tappin's first coach, 1930. The coach is parked outside his bungalow in St John's Road. It was said to be the last word in comfort, being a show model; its bodywork was built on a Thorneycroft chassis. *(JJ)*

The service of thanksgiving at the tenth anniversary of the British Legion, Sunday 14 July 1931. The men's branch of the Legion paraded from their headquarters in St John's Road through the town to the Bull Croft, accompanied by the Cholsey Branch, local Territorials under Bill Field, the Mayor (T.E. Wells) and several members of the Corporation, Girl Guides and Boy Scouts. As they passed the war memorial Colonel J.R. Wyndham, of St John's House, lay a wreath. They then moved on to the Bull Croft, where the women Legionaries had assembled. The rector of Brightwell, the Revd F.B. Girling, conducted the service. Afterwards tea was given to all those who had taken part in the pavilion, St John's Road. *(DB)*

The Market Place, 1932. The Corn Exchange was being used as a cinema, known as the Exchange Cinema. During the interval a slide was projected on to the screen advertising accommodation at The Fat Ox for tramps. The lane next to the Corn Exchange was then known as Little Lane. The four-storey building next to the lane was Franklin and Gale's auctioneers. Frank Jenkins's Garage was next, which had two petrol pumps; when cars were filled with petrol the hose had to be stretched across the pavement. Wallingford Post Office comes next; it was opened in 1893 and closed in 1936. Both Jenkins's and the Post Office sites are now occupied by Boots the Chemist's. After the post office stood Victor Chadd's tobacconist's shop. The tall building on the right was Barclays Bank. *(COS)*

Thames Street, 1932, looking towards the High Street. On the left is the Drill Hall, previously Gerrard's Hall. In 1932 it was being used by the 4th Battalion Royal Berkshire Regiment, a Territorial Battery; they were based here from the 1920s until 1968. Jack Laker was manager of the hall. Next door there were three terraced cottages, demolished in the 1960s. The site is now the Thames Street car park. *(COS)*

Mayor's Sunday, *c.* 1932. The Mayor, accompanied by the town aldermen, councillors, clergy, police and the town band would parade through the main streets. Among those pictured are the Revd H.P. Bowen, Rector of St Mary's Church; Horace Walters, Mayor; Leonard Shepherd of Stone Hall; Town Clerk, Francis Hedges, who lived at the Old Brewery House; and Henry Thomas Marcham, mace bearer. *(DB)*

The Co-op Christmas Party, St Leonard's Church Hall, 1933. Front row, left to right: Gladys Stevens, Jaclyn Jordan, Phillis Green (later Mrs Cameron), Jose Goff, -?-, Frances Stevens, -?-, Rose Bennett, Stan Wells, Margaret Wells. Third row: Kathleen Bennett (later Mrs Walden), -?-, Miss Jordan, Peggy Jeskins (later Mrs Wheeler), Father Christmas (name unknown), -?-, Connie Leaver, Elizabeth Bennett (later Mrs Warwick), Evelyn Rose, Joyce Rose. Second row: Miss Green, Linda Stevens, Master Doe, Peggy Hobbs, Winnie Becket, Mrs Hockley, Joan Baldwin, Beryl Doe, Master Herman, -?-, -?-, Dora Wells. Back row: Mrs Green, Daisy Bolton, Evelyn Gard, -?-, -?-, -?-, Master Eldridge, Master Stevens, -?-, -?-, B. Hobbs, Mrs Hobbs. *(BW)*

Armistice Day, 1932. Mr Leonard Shepherd, Mayor of Wallingford, laying a wreath at the war memorial. Being a schoolday there were a large number of children and their teachers present, along with the men's and women's branches of the Wallingford British Legion. Also in attendance were the Territorials, aldermen and town councillors. The 'Last Post' was played by Private Watters. The ceremony was held on 11 November, not the nearest Sunday to the 11th, as is the practice today. *(DB)*

A retirement presentation to Mr W. Chilvers at Walter Wilder's, Crowmarsh, in 1934. Left to right: Frank Wilder, Walter Wilder (presenting the gifts), and Percy Wilder and his son (with the scarf). The man with the dirty face behind the chair is Bill Tame. Frank Wilder made the pattern for the cast-iron chimneys used on the *Margaret* and *Noreen* steam engines; Mr Chilvers was the moulder who cast those chimneys. *(BT)*

The St John's Ambulance Brigade outside the fire station, *c.* 1934. The picture was taken before the fire station doors were changed to a square-shaped doorway. Those pictured include Olive Emmett, Aggie Rolls, Mr Polley and Bill Bolton. *(OR)*

The Whitecross Hotel, Winterbrook, *c.* 1935. For much of the nineteenth century it was the home of the Arnould family. *(DB)*

John Hoddinott's public address van, *c.* 1935. The picture was taken near Harris's Garages off the High Street, which stood opposite the four shops near the Bull Croft. The houses behind the van were demolished in the early 1960s. John Hoddinott had an electrical shop in Wallingford from 1931; when John died the business was taken over by his son, Peter, who managed the shop until it closed in 1987. *(PH)*

The Keep the Country Beautiful, a petrol filling station and café, 1938. The KCB was situated at the junction of old Benson Lane and the Old London Road, right in the middle of RAF Benson. The petrol station was opened on 22 July 1931. Mr Oakley was the first owner; he later sold the premises to Major R. Horsfield on 1 March 1935. Being so near an RAF base, life at the KCB was not without excitement, particularly one day when an aircraft that was taking off removed the café chimney. Because of extensions to the runways on the airfield, the café was moved into Benson in July 1942, and the petrol station was closed down on August Bank Holiday 1942. *(DB)*

Maypole dancing performed for the Coronation Pageant, May 1937. All the performers in the Pageant paraded from the Kine Croft through the principal streets of the town to the Bull Croft, where they then performed the Pageant in front of a very large crowd. After the performance the Mayor, Horace Walters, gave a short speech of thanks to all the performers. Tea was provided for over 400 children in the Masonic Hall, and each child was presented with a Coronation mug. The Mayoress, meanwhile, was presented with a bouquet by Pamela Ansell. Many children entered the competition for the best-arranged May garlands. The winner was Pamela Jolly; in second place came Joyce Crook, with Norah Simmonds third. The prize-winners for the best-decorated cottages were: (first prize) Mr Perry of 8 South View, (second) Mr Tubb of Goldsmith's Lane and (third) Mrs Scudds of 6 St John's Road and Mrs Ansell of 51 St John's Road. *(DB)*

Clifford Atwell at his mayor-making, 1937, touching the ceremonial mace, held for him by the outgoing Mayor, Horace Walters. The Town Clerk, Francis R. Hedges, can be seen standing between them; the Revd Mr Bowen is the clergyman looking on. The picture was taken in the Town Hall, and the three paintings on the wall are of (left to right): George Dunlop Leslie RA, James Hayllar and Henry Hawkins. *(JA)*

A scene from the Coronation Pageant, 6 May 1937. The pageant was called 'Scenes from Merry England', written and produced by Percy Turner. It was performed in the Bull Croft and portrayed the signing of the Magna Carta. It also included the ladies of the court performing for King John, a masque depicting Robin Hood, followed by Maypole dancing by the village children. King John was played by Colonel M. Morrell of Newnham Croft, Crowmarsh. His queen, Mrs Haggie of Shillingford, can be seen with him at the head of the procession. The barons were Maj Hinton of Turner's Court, Don Lester of St Peter's Street, Miss Pamela Hedges of the Castle and Mr Frost of Benson. The court retinue were Rosemary Hedges of the Castle, Arthur Shepherd of Flint House, Miss Tickner of St Mary's Street, Miss G. Brown of Castle Street, Mrs P. Ayres of Reading Road and Charles Allan of the High Street. Robin Hood was played by Mrs Redfern of St Lucien's. Maid Marion was played by Miss Diane Hedges of the Castle. The monk was Keith Jenkins. Ladies of the court included S. Johnson, N. Ford and Joyce Munday, all of Station Road, Hilda Shepherd of Flint House and E. Field of St John's Road. The freemen's pages were played by Master W. Walter of Highgrove, Master Geoffrey Ponking of The Nook and Master John Atwell of Croft Road. Finally, the Jester was played by Mr J. Andrew of Westminster Bank. *(DB)*

The 1st Wallingford Ranger Company, George VI's Coronation, 6 May 1937. One of the prize-winning fancy dress displays. Back row, left to right: Olive Emmett, Hilda Shepherd, Freda Bartlett. Middle row: Daisy Brown, Joan Tarry, Daisy Rowe, Daisy Wells. Front row: Phyllis Morris, Molly Ford, -?-. (OR)

George V's Silver Jubilee, 6 May 1935. The crowds are gathered for the service of thanksgiving in the Market Place. The Revd Mr Bowen conducted the service; the Mayor (Harold Lovelock) and Corporation attended the service. John Hoddinott's public-address van is to the right of the Town Hall. There was a sports day in the Bull Croft and a free film was shown at the Regal Cinema for the children. There was also a tea for the unemployed at the Conservative Hall, plus an old people's and children's tea. The King gave a speech on the wireless which was broadcast from the Town Hall by Mr Hoddinott. The day finished with a bonfire and fireworks. (PH)

Wallingford Territorials at Churn Rifle Range, Blewbury, *c.* 1936. The corporal is instructing the five soldiers on how to fire a Lewis gun. The man second from the right is Cyril Beasley. *(WB)*

The 4th Battalion Royal Berkshire Territorials at the Drill Hall, Thames Street, 1936. Back row, left to right: ? Westbrook, ? Allan, Fred Lovegrove (killed 1940), H. Frewin, Jim Brant, J. Hester, ? Goodenough and B. Brown. Second row: -?-, Sid Hobbs, -?-, B. Buckle, -?-, Reginald 'Snowy' Whichelow (killed 1940), Charlie Tame, Cyril 'Basher' Beasley (wounded 1940), ? Herman, H. Bill, ? Tubb and Jack Laker (PoW 1940–5). Front row: ? Griffin, George Strudwick (transferred to the Commandos 1942), A. Atkins, ? Barlow, Bert Field, Douglas Gale (CO), -?-, F. Simmonds, Harry Edwards (killed 1940), Freddie Spooner, -?-. *(DB)*

The Wallingford Territorials at their
annual camp on Salisbury Plain, 1938.
As young as these boys look, they were all
to be called up one year later. The man
on the left at the front is Sidney Moody,
who served right through the war in
North Africa, Sicily and Italy. Two of the
others are ? Belcher and ? Coggins from
Benson. *(SM)*

The Wallingford Territorials, B Company,
Royal Berkshire Regiment were called up
at the start of the war in September 1939.
They were stationed overnight in the Corn
Exchange. The man on guard is Private
Bartlett. The next day they marched to the
railway station in Wallingford and left for
Reading, much as they had done in 1914.
They spent four months in training at
Newbury and were inspected by King
George VI in early January 1940. Two
weeks later they arrived in France, when
they disembarked at Le Havre. The French
dockers were on strike and the weather
was very cold, but there were no extra
blankets so each soldier had to manage
with just one. *(DB)*

A flood in The Street, Crowmarsh, in 1940 caused by a rapid thaw of snow on the hills above Crowmarsh. The winter of 1939/40 was very cold all over Europe; in fact, one soldier in the Royal Berkshires died of exposure in France. The wall on the left is part of Newnham Manor, and on the right are the Dormer Cottages, which in 1940 were in very poor condition. They continued to be occupied until the early 1970s, when they were finally demolished. *(DB)*

Wallingford's new bathing place, *c.* 1936. The diving boards and the building were opened on 22 May 1935 by the Mayoress, Mrs H. Lovelock. The Mayor was unable to attend because of a heavy cold, although it was thought around the town that he stayed away to avoid having to do the first dive. After a speech by the Mayoress, there was a diving display by professional divers from London. *(DB)*

Ice House Hill, Crowmarsh, *c.* 1938. It was so named because an icehouse that belonged to Mongewell House used to stand on the island near the South Stoke turn. In June 1974, despite opposition from the District Council and the Protection for Rural England, this peaceful scene was destroyed when the road was widened. All that remains today is the road. *(DB)*

The official opening of the Bull Croft took place on Wednesday 12 August 1914. It was overshadowed by the declaration of war the previous week (4 August), and so all the opening celebrations were cancelled. The Bull Croft, which was to have been opened by the Mayor of Reading, Alderman G. Field (an old Wallingfordian), was instead opened by the Mayor's wife, Mrs P. de M. Cavell. On being handed the key she ceremonially unlocked the gates to the park. After a speech by the Mayor, the large crowd sang the national anthem and then dispersed. The Bull Croft, once Holy Trinity Priory, was given to the borough by Mr Powys-Lybbe. It consisted of some 14 acres (5.7 hectares). The gift also included Croft House in Castle Street. Its lawns, with a monkey tree growing in the middle, can be seen on the east side of the park today. The property is rented out by the Corporation, thus providing an income with which to maintain the Bull Croft. Between the wars, sheep were allowed to graze in the park. For a number of years a captured German field gun stood in front of the tree in the centre of the picture. *(DB)*

Chapter Five

1941 to 1950

The Thames, frozen at Shillingford Bridge, 1942. Harry Grant of Warborough, brave soul, was cycling across on the ice. A shortage of coal and the many power-cuts made the winters of the 1940s, which were in any case often very cold, even worse. *(DB)*

American forces marching through Wallingford at the end of the Second World War. There were a large number of Americans stationed in and around the town. Many engineers were stationed at Howbery Park; the remains of their Nissen huts can still be seen there. More troops were stationed in the town itself. *(LS)*

This concrete model can still be seen in the beech woods at Highmoor. It was made by 343 US engineers, stationed here during the Second World War, and is often visited by American veterans. *(DB)*

Johnny Wilding was an American from New York who
served in the Royal Canadian Air Force in 1944, flying
Halifax bombers. On the morning of 9 September 1944 he
took off with his crew for an early morning raid in support
of Allied troops around Le Havre. Because of low cloud, the
raid was aborted. Part of the bomb load was jettisoned in
the English Channel to bring the aircraft down to its
landing weight. Somewhere south of Wallingford, however,
a fire started in the port engines. The skipper, Johnny
Wilding, decided to abandon the aircraft. He told the crew
to bail out, but the bomber was now near Wallingford and
there was a danger it would crash on the town, so he and
Sergeant Andrews, an RAF man from Wales, decided to
stay onboard and steer away from Wallingford. They
crashed in fields just across the river from the town. The
concussion from the explosion broke shop windows half a
mile away. Two roads on the council estate were named in
memory of Wilding and Andrews, and a cairn was erected
where these two roads meet. *(LS)*

John Heaton (right), in Burma, *c.* 1943. John served with the RAF during the Second World War in
Burma and Malaya. Here he has been fishing using hand grenades – throwing them into a river to stun
the fish. A Lancastrian by birth, John lived most of his life in Wallingford. He married Joan Young in
December 1941 while stationed at RAF Benson and working for the Wessex Southern Electricity Board.
His promise to bring home a wave in a bottle for a small boy each time he went on holiday will always
be remembered. *(JHN)*

An aerial view of Castle House, *c.* 1941. The circular and rectangular patches are flower borders. Just below the curved garden path is Castle Lane, which forms the dog-leg at the top left of the picture. *(CC)*

Wallingford's Voluntary Aid Detachment, *c.* 1945. This picture was taken in the gardens of the three cottages that once stood here; they were later demolished and the site was used for the Thames Street car park. Front row, left to right: -?-, Lou Crook, -?-, J. Arthur Johnstone (Mayor) and Captain Downs MC; the lady at the end of the row is Bertha Ayres. In the back row the lady third from the right is Marian Coxe. *(LC)*

Mr Gardener, a railway employee, was very keen on topiary; this rider is an excellent example of his craft. The topiary could be seen on the branch line between Wallingford and Cholsey in the 1940s, although there were some examples here that dated back to before the First World War. *(COS)*

Wallingford Victory Parade, 30 July 1945. These two soldiers are part of the fancy dress parade, but they seem to have called in at all the pubs on its route. This was one of three official holidays that Wallingford had for VE (Victory in Europe) Day, the others being when Germany surrendered on 8 May, 9 May and again on 30 July for the official celebration. *(PB)*

The children's fancy dress parade in the Bull Croft during the VE celebrations, 30 July 1945. The children had a full sports programme, and there was bowling for a pig. In the evening there was dancing in an area prepared and illuminated by the RAF, who also provided the music. *(TC)*

The winners of the children's fancy dress parade outside the Pavilion in the Bull Croft during the VE Day celebrations on 30 July. The prize-winners were: (under 5s) Patricia Kiddie (first), Patricia Andrews (second) and Zena Lansley (third); (5–8) Tony Crabbe (first), P. Febre (second) and Patsy Walder (third); (8–11) Shirley Pearman (first), Kathleen Crabbe (second). *(IA)*

A family group of Polish refugees at the Camp for Displaced Persons at Howbery Park, *c.* 1947. The families were housed in Nissen huts left by the American Engineers who were stationed here during the Second World War. The families had all been repatriated or rehoused in this country by 1950, when Howbery Park was purchased by the Government for the new Hydraulics Research Organisation. *(GM)*

The secondary entrance to Howbery Park, *c.* 1948. The site was being used by the National Assistance Board as a hostel for Polish refugees. The Poles staying here were either repatriated or chose to live in Britain. By 1950 they had left Howbery Park and the Hydraulics Research Organisation took over the site, at which time the elm trees that line this drive were all cut down; the huts on the left have only recently been demolished. *(DB)*

The Thames in flood, March 1947. This view is of the road going to Upper Wharf, past The Town Arms. The 1947 flood was the third highest on record for the Thames (only the floods of 1809 and 1894 were higher). As a comparison, in 1947 13,572 million gallons a day flowed through Teddington Weir; in 1894 it was 20,236 million gallons. *(JA)*

The 1947 flood at Wallingford Bridge. The flood peaked on 20 March; this photograph was taken the day before. This time the flood did not reach the High Street, as it had done in 1894. None the less, the houses in Lower Wharf were badly flooded, as were the kitchens and outdoor toilets of some properties in St Leonard's Lane; as a bizarre result of this some children were able to feed swans from their bedroom windows. *(PB)*

The Lamb Corner, *c.* 1939. The policeman on point duty seems to be controlling a level of traffic enviably modest by today's standards. The shop just before the George Hotel is the Wallingford Wine and Spirit Company; Mr Percy Carstairs was the manager. In 1979 the Lamb Hotel was converted into a centre for antiques. The building on the right with the delivery boy standing outside was the World Stores. On the policeman's left arm can be seen a black-and-white armband, indicating that he was on duty. *(DB)*

The rear of the Lamb Hotel, 1948. The hotel was originally leased by Trust House Ltd from Wallingford Brewery in 1926. At the time this picture was taken, the hotel had been refurbished and modernised to plans drawn up by the Brewery's Managing Director, Major Rudkins. The photograph is taken from the hotel garage from which Horace Walters ran his taxi business. The car in the picture is probably one of his. *(DB)*

Wallingford football team outside the Pavilion, the Bull Croft, 1949. Back row, left to right: John Crabbe, Sid Ansell, Derrick Giles, ? Bond, Ken Castle, Tony Colquhoun and John Andrews. Middle row: Cecil Low and Wilf Thomas. Front row: Johnny Low, M. Harris, Den Gomm, William Blake, Jeff Davis and Ken Blissett. *(KC)*

Wallingford Girls' School, 1950. Back row, left to right: -?-, -?-, Barbara Fox, Marion Sadler, Sheila Tilling, Patricia Kiddie, Sally Kent, Fay Kent, Margaret Crook. Middle row: Valerie Palmer, Beverly Clayton, -?-, Zena Lansley, -?-, -?-, Lillian Painter, -?-, Margaret Crabbe. Front row: -?-, Janet Iles, Annette Derrick, Heather Conner, Gillian Constable, Geraldine Griffin. *(MG)*

Chapter Six

1951 to 1960

George Atkins, an old Wallingfordian and manager of the Regal Cinema, would often use the foyer of the Regal for various displays. This one, from the early 1950s, was to promote Army recruitment. It was not unknown for him to pay for repairs to his car with free cinema tickets. *(GA)*

The last R.J. and H. Wilder traction engine to be rebuilt at their Wallingford iron foundry. It was rebuilt in the early 1950s by Bill Tame, who worked for Wilder's most of his working life. Bill and his brother Harold made two model traction engines which they used to plough their garden in Wantage Road for many years. *(BT)*

Wallingford Railway staff, *c.* 1954. Back row, left to right: -?-, George Polley, Bill Bolton, Charles Minty (driver), Fred Jolley, Ken Pearce, Bill Hyde and Bob Barefoot. Front row: Ken Mitchell, John Ashfield, Jack Merritt, Joyce Munday (booking clerk), E. Davis (station master), Olive Rumble, Mr Evans, Jack Cope and Paddy Roach. *(CT)*

The box office of the Regal Cinema, Christmas 1950. At the end of each showing the national anthem would be played, as can be seen advertised at the bottom of the programme board. In the early 1950s there were few homes with a television, so a night out at the cinema was a regular thing for many families. At this showing of *Cinderella* there were long queues, as was usually the case. *(RA)*

Below: The Wallingford Brewery and Mineral Water Company staff outing to Margate, 1951. Back row, left to right: Mr Percy George (Tappin's coach driver), Ron Dodd, Maurice Luckett, Joyce Dodd (née Bullock), K. Philips, Don Brown, Ted Hobbs, Den Polley, Rene Strange, Mr Strange, Ray Kent, Mrs Page, Mr J. Page, Mrs Percy King, Les Baber, Wally Emery, Ernest Strudwick. Middle row: Mr Coles, Mrs Coles, Dennis James, Dorothy Brown, Walter Luckett, Percy King (manager of the Mineral Water Company), Phillis Emery. Front row: Ray Coles, Johnny Hobbs, Avis Hobbs, Alley Baber, Miss Emery, Peter Baber and Alan Coles. *(LS)*

The Lamb Corner, *c.* 1952. The shops on the left side are C.P. Smith's sweetshop; Brown Brothers' tailor's; the Southern Electricity Board; Hunt's Seed and Corn Merchant's; the Lamb Hotel; Ferguson's Wine Merchant's; and the George Hotel. On the right are the Municipal Offices (formerly the Red Lion Hotel); Martin and Silver's draper's shop; Vertigen's sweet shop; Jack O'Newbury's drycleaner's; and the Copper Kettle café. The latter would eventually be converted into Baylis's supermarket. This right-hand side of the High Street, from the corner of St Martin's Street almost up to Goldsmith's Lane, was demolished in the 1960s with little thought given to preserving any of the buildings (as often happened in the 1960s and '70s). In getting rid of the squalor we also lost the picturesque. *(DB)*

St Mary's Street, looking towards the Market Place, *c.* 1952. The Dolphin public house is on the left; Millward's shoeshop is next, followed by The White Hart public house. Dawson the cobbler's is on the right, followed by Doug Selwood's hairdresser's. Strange's grocer's shop was next door, next to Tilly's butcher's. *(DB)*

One of the floats in the Coronation illuminated river pageant, 5 June 1953. Because of bad weather the pageant was postponed until the Saturday after Coronation Day (2 June 1953). *(JJ)*

Croft Road Coronation tea party, St John's School hall. Back row, left to right: Rhoda Becket (née Polley), Ivy Corral (née Scudds), Dolly Kent, Alice Elliot, Eve Woodley, Sylvia Bussey, Mrs Howard, Audrey Shorter, Joyce Crook, Mrs Ely, Laura Iles. Middle row: David Becket, Catherine Becket, Michael Woodley, -?-, Ernie Nunn, Alan Hill, Margaret Crook, Norma Howard, Carol Shorter, Anne Elliot, Robert Crook, Harold Crook, William Hobbs. Front row: John Corral, -?-, Peter Howard, Maureen Bussey, Robert Elliot, Mary Elliot, Janet Iles, Pamela Iles, -?-, Anne Nunn. *(DB)*

Below: The ox roast in the Kine Croft, Coronation Day, 2 June 1953. The men wearing the white coats are local butchers. The one on the right is Mr Alfred C. Lester of St Peter's Street; on his right is Frank Bosley of St Mary's Street; next is George Hobbs; and on his right is Mrs Hockley. The man on the left of the picture is John Wright, with Mr Polley in front (with the pipe). The celebrations started in the early evening with a parade of decorated vehicles. Twenty-six vehicles took part, including several horse-drawn, and a number of decorated bicycles. The winner of the trade group were Messrs Pettit, something they had managed to achieve for a number of years (going back to 1932). Prizes for the decorated bicycles went to Peter Ashby (first), Jennifer Tappin (second) and J. Hoddinott (third). Winners in the children's fancy dress were (ten–fifteen years) Clive and Johnny Hobbs (Cricketers – first prize), Ann Lester (Gypsy – second prize) and Tony Morris (Guardsman – third prize). The visitors' prizes were won by Ken Passey of Benson (Circus – first prize) and Bert Passey of Benson (Covered Wagon – second prize). After each resident had received a slice of ox meat a beacon was lit, followed by community singing until midnight around a camp fire provided by the Scouts. *(DB)*

Coronation street party, St Nicholas Road, 5 June 1953. Because of the bad weather the party was held on the Saturday instead of the actual day of the Coronation (the previous Wednesday). The lady on the right with the handbag is the Mayoress, Mrs Simmonds; on her left is her daughter, Mrs Butcher, and on her right is Mrs Herman. The lady with the tall hat is Mrs Tilly; on her right is Mrs Waldern, with Mrs Turner standing next to her. Behind her Mrs Waldern is Sylvia Turner. The tall lady behind Mrs Herman is Mrs Fisher; the old lady in the centre of the picture is Mrs Young; the baby in the pram is Richard Heaton, Mrs Young's grandson. In addition to this street party, another was held on the same day at St John's School hall (see page 110). *(JA)*

A Coronation cake made by Rose Hobbs for the first St Nicholas Road street party. This was thought to be one of the best of all the Coronation cakes made for the various street parties. *(EW)*

Winners of one of the fancy dress competitions in the Wallingford pageant, August 1955. Left to right: Iris Simmonds (née Mann), Joyce Huntley and Pearl Larkman. The winners of the children's fancy dress competition were: (4–6 years) Christine Leigh (gypsy – first), Ian Wheeler (TV set – second) and Elizabeth Aves (Bo-Peep – third); (6–8 years) Jennifer Longbottom (No Strikes – first), Cynthia Fish (Honolulu – second), Neale Bussey (highwayman – third). The decorated bicycles competition was won by Graham Wells, with Christopher Aves coming second. (JH)

A scene from the Wallingford pageant, August 1955. The pageant was produced by Frances Curtis and consisted of nine scenes from Wallingford's history, starting with a Regency scene from 1810. Each scene went back in time, finishing with the town's being sacked by the Vikings in 1006. The scene here is of Queen Matilda discussing the terms of a peace treaty with King Stephen in 1141. Matilda was played by A. Rawlinson and Stephen by D. Hutt, Tony Barr-Taylor played the Duke of Normandy and the monks were played by A.J. Dean, A. Wilder, E. Pyke, E.V. Naish, G. Severn, C.H. Simmons, A.C. Pocock, C. Goodall and C. Chapman. (DB)

A scene from the Wallingford pageant, August 1955. The scene is a tournament at Wallingford Castle held by Piers Gaveston for Edward II, which included jousting. The riders were from the South Oxfordshire Hunt. Piers Gaveston was played by R. Richmond, Edward II by John Atwell, the Cheapjack by J. Collyer and Warwick by Guy Severn. (LC)

Clifford Atwell, being presented with a case on his retirement as Headmaster of Wallingford Boys' Council School, St John's Road, in 1950. On the left of the picture is Arthur Dean, his successor as headmaster. When St John's School first took in girls, Mr Dean, the headmaster, was very apprehensive about teaching girls. The first day of mixed classes, he made a remark that there were no flowers in the classroom and did this mean they did not like their headmaster. The next day the room was full of flowers, and his concern about teaching girls changed instantly. *(DB)*

Wallingford station, *c.* 1954. The station was opened on 7 July 1866. The original intention had been to join up with the Watlington line, but this was abandoned because of lack of funds. Finally, in December 1872, GWR (the Great Western Railway) took over the line. The train would drive to Moulsford, but when the latter was closed in 1893 Cholsey was opened. In 1958/9 the author travelled from Wallingford to Cholsey each weekday; as there were so few passengers early in the morning the train driver would often wait for him. The train is seen here passing by the Egerton Road allotments. *(DB)*

The last run of the Wallingford to Cholsey train ('the Bunk'), 15 June 1959 (the goods service continued until September 1965). The Mayor of Wallingford, Clifford Atwell, is shaking hands with the Stationmaster, Mr E. Davis; looking between them is Mr Lester and behind Mr Davis is 'Tot' Simmonds, with David Calvin-Thomas next to her. By the Mayor's side is Mr Smith, a former mayor of Wallingford. *(JC-T)*

Crowds waiting for Queen Elizabeth II to appear on the Town Hall balcony during her visit to Wallingford, 2 November 1956. Flags and bunting decorated the route that the Queen took through the town. The Market Place was a blaze of colour. The RAF and local uniformed organisations lined the route. When the Queen arrived she was met by the Town Council and the Commanding Officer of RAF Benson. She was presented with a bouquet of freesias by Pamela Iles. The Mayor, J.O. Johnstone, gave a Loyal Address, which was followed with a speech from the Queen. After unveiling a commemorative plaque of her visit to Wallingford she signed the Visitors' Book and then left to visit the Hydraulics Research Station at Howbery Park. *(JH)*

Queen Elizabeth II inspecting the RAF Guard of Honour on her visit to Wallingford and Howbery Park, 2 November 1956. At Howbery she met the Director of the Hydraulics Research Station, Sir Claude Inglis, and was then shown around several of the physical models in the main hall by members of staff, who included R.C. Russell, Jim Ham, Reg Drew, Mac Wilkie, Les Jeffrey and Harry Dedow. From Howbery the Queen went on to RAF Benson for a short visit. She then proceeded to Englefield House to have tea with the Lord Lieutenant of Berkshire, Mr H.A. Benyon. *(DB)*

The inside of the Regal Cinema, *c.* 1960. The cinema opened in 1934. In 1944, during a performance of the Jimmy Cagney movie *Yankee Doodle Dandy*, the curtains caught fire and the cinema had to be evacuated. Each member of the audience was given free admission two nights later. When *Rock around the Clock* was shown in Wallingford, George Atkins (the Manager) asked for a policeman to be on duty in the cinema because he feared a repeat of what teenagers in London had done – dancing in the aisles and breaking up the seating. Mr Honey, a special constable, duly attended; a man in his late sixties, he managed to sleep through every performance. But his presence must have had some effect, as there was no trouble. *(GA)*

The old 'Bunk Arch' railway bridge on the Hithercroft Road in the course of being demolished, *c.* 1960. *(DB)*

Chapter Seven

1961 to 1970

The Gangbusters, Wallingford's own pop group. They were very popular during the 1960s and '70s, and even today they still are getting regular gigs (possibly to supplement their pensions . . .). They were first known as the Club Six Rhythm Group, but after a year or two they changed their name to the Gangbusters. After appearing at the Adelphi Theatre, Slough, in 1963 they were spotted by the recording agent Michael Collier, and as a result a record was eventually released. They played alongside such well-known acts of the day as Gerry and the Pacemakers, Bert Weedon and Kenny Ball. Left to right: Michael Coxe (drummer), Johnny Hobbs, Johnny Evans and John Jeskins. *(MC)*

Wallingford Carnival, 1964. After parading through the town the floats assemble in the Kine Croft. This is the Hydraulic Research Station Float. Some of the people on it are Brian Robins, Peter Baber, Valerie Cope, John Jones, Madeline Potter, Carol Warne, Ivor Shaw and George Clarke. The lorry was loaned from Bushell's Haulage Company, whose director, Trevor Davis, worked for Hydraulic Research as a draftsman. *(BR)*

An aerial view of Howbery Park, 1970. The Reynolds Building is in the centre. It was erected in three stages, the third stage was finished in 1962. The Manor House is at the top end of the Reynolds Building; the building to the right of the Manor House is a Wave Basin made of cedar wood. Wallingford can be seen in the distance; Maltsters is the large building at the top of the picture. Some of the Second World War Nissen huts can be seen around the site. *(HR Wallingford Ltd)*

An aerial view of Wallingford, looking south, *c.* 1970. Much of the new development of the period can be seen in this picture. Goldsmith's Lane is on the extreme right, running past Hunt's warehouse, the building with all the skylights in the roof. The entrance to the Waitrose car park is next; a row of Victorian terraced houses was knocked down to make way for the entrance. Beansheaf Terrace, the row of buildings after the car park entrance, lost half their gardens to give more space to the car park. St Alban's car park can be seen bottom right, built in the gardens of St Alban's House. Waitrose, the large building top centre, was built in 1974. Again, houses were removed to make way for the supermarket. At this time parking in the Market Place is still allowed, but this would end with the pedestrianisation of the area in 1978. *(PH)*

Wallingford Rowing Club, with their impressive display of trophies, 1963. Wallingford has had a strong tradition in rowing ever since the 1880s, with the Fairy and Albion Rowing Clubs. The present rowing club was formed in 1947. In 1953 they purchased the Castle Priory Malthouse, their present boathouse. The club has had great success both nationally and internationally, the 1980s being perhaps their best years so far. During that period the club won 11 gold, 10 silver and 7 bronze medals at the National Championships. The club members in this picture are, back row, left to right: Mark ?, Mike Coxe, David Luker, Ted Field, Carl Purchase, Norman Williams, Bob Elliot, John Broadbent, Len Herring, Chris Povell and Nick ? (a New Zealander). Front row: Colin Cusack and Ralph Daniels, both of whom coxed various crews. *(MC)*

Opposite, bottom: The view from the top of the Associated British Maltsters building, reputed to be the largest of its type in Europe, and built close to the site of the old 'Bunk Arch' in 1958. The building was known locally as Wallingford Cathedral; it was finally demolished in 2001. *(JA)*

Wilder's Wharf, 1964. In the 1940s on the left-hand side of this road there were a large number of old steam-driven agricultural machines and traction engines, along with several shepherds' huts on which children from the neighbourhood would play. The white house in the distance was occupied by Mr Stamp, a marine dealer. *(KC)*

Some of the old workhouse buildings, St Mary's Hospital, *c*. 1968. All of these buildings were demolished in 1982. In the 1960s the Adventure Youth Club used some of them. The club was run by David Calvin-Thomas. *(COS)*

The main entrance to St Mary's Hospital, *c*. 1968. In 1930 the Workhouse was renamed the Berkshire County Council Institution. However, this did nothing to lessen the fear that the elderly had of ending up in the workhouse, a fear that continued into the 1960s. During the Second World War part of the hospital was used as a maternity unit. When the National Health Service was formed in 1948, the hospital was renamed St Mary's. In October 1982 it was closed and the land sold off for £1.75 million, for housing development. *(COS)*

The gardens and buildings of St Mary's Hospital, *c.* 1968. The gardens at St Mary's were always very well kept. In the 1960s the building in the centre of the picture was converted into flats for the nursing staff. *(DB)*

A mercy flight for Mrs Kathleen O'Loughlin, 20 January 1963. She was about to give birth to her first baby, but because of the heavy snow that winter her husband could not get her to St George's Maternity Hospital, Wallingford. The O'Loughlin's family GP, Dr Andrew Miller of Benson, contacted RAF Benson, which provided a helicopter to get Kathleen there. The picture shows the baby being carried to the hospital. St George's was first opened in December 1951 (by the Mayor, Mrs F.F. Simmonds). *(JH)*

Ban the Arrow, a display from the 1964 Wallingford Carnival. Wallingford has a fine tradition of carnivals which continues to the present day. *(JJ)*

Opposite, bottom: The Municipal Offices, the High Street, September 1962, the year they were put up for sale. The offices were moved to Stone Hall. The building was once the old Red Lion Commercial Hotel, which closed in 1935. The landlord, Cecil B. Low, moved across the road and became landlord of The Beehive. The supermarket chain Key Markets had a store built on the site of the Red Lion.

Two lorries jammed for over an hour in the High Street outside the George Hotel, 15 June 1962. Such scenes as this were becoming all too common in Wallingford in the 1960s and '70s. A Wallingford lady once had her nose broken by a lorry's wing-mirror while she was walking along the pavement. These traffic problems weren't relieved until the Wallingford bypass was finally built in 1992, after sixty years of promises. *(DB)*

The paddling pool and swimming pool, 1969. The swimming pool was built next to the old bathing place on the river bank in 1953 as part of the coronation celebrations. The paddling pool was opened in 1955 to celebrate the town's 800 years as a borough.

Armistice Day, 1963. The 1st Wallingford Girl Guides on parade, led by Captain Bowles. In the front row, behind her, are Cynthia Huntley (whose father Geoffrey Bradburn was Mayor of Wallingford) and Sally Jose. In the background can be seen Frank Jenkins's garage.

Chapter Eight

1971 to 1980

The unveiling of the Hawkins Drinking Fountain, by David Calvin-Thomas, in August 1979. This drinking fountain was originally erected in 1885 to replace a hand-pump. In 1921 Sidney Hawkins, the Wallingford draper, paid to have it moved to the Bull Croft in order to make room for the new War Memorial. Mrs Jean Calvin-Thomas is standing behind her husband, David. *(JC-T)*

Wallingford Market
Place, from the tower
of St Mary's Church,
c. 1970. The Friday
market is being held;
covered stalls can be
seen in the centre of
the picture. The white
concrete building in
the centre replaced
those demolished to
widen St Martin's
Street. Thankfully
this building was
given a new façade
more in keeping with
the town's
architecture in 2000.
(MC)

The Regal Cinema, just before it closed in 1973. The film advertised was the very last to be shown. The owner of the Regal was John Watsham of Bloxham. George Atkins was the manager. He had worked there since 1934, when the Regal was first opened, having previously worked at the Exchange Cinema until it closed in 1934. Florence Jones was the head usherette; she started at the cinema in 1947. *(DB)*

Opposite, top: The pedestrianisation of the Market Place, November 1978. This caused considerable traffic disruption and affected the takings of shops in the Market Place. *(DB)*

Opposite, bottom: A further picture of the pedestrianisation of the Market Place, November 1979. The white building to the left of the Town Hall was Jenkins's garage, here in the process of being converted into Boots the Chemist. The hamburger van on the left is there more for the benefit of the workmen than the general public. *(DB)*

St George's Hospital staff, January 1972. Left to right: Sister O'Shea, Joy Harvey, Mrs Johnson, Mrs Hammond, Mrs Marsden (Matron), Sister Rowlands, Diane Billings, Madge Fuller, Iris Johnston, Rose Davis, Jackie Davis, Billy Benham, Edna Blake and Dorothy Farmer. Rowlands Close is named in memory of Sister Rowlands. *(JH)*

Wallingford Fire Brigade fighting a blaze at Lupton and Morton Furnishings, Croft Road, *c.* 1972. Presumably the fire has been dealt with, as everyone seems very relaxed. These buildings were once part of Wallingford's tannery. *(WFB)*

Boots the Chemist opened their store in the Market Place, Wallingford, on 4 October 1979. Their very first customer was Mrs Diana Pearce, wife of Crowmarsh policeman Patrick (Pat); she is being presented with several Boots tokens by the store manager. *(BL)*

Wallingford Post Office, November 1979. Opened in 1936, it is one of the few post offices in the country to have Edward VIII's royal cipher over the main door. The post office was declared open on 11 December 1936 by the High Steward of the Borough, Maj Sir Ralph Glyn. The actual opening ceremony was held in the Town Hall. *(DB) Below:* Edward VIII's royal cipher above the main door of Wallingford Post Office. Because Edward VIII reigned for only a few months (January to December 1936), there were very few of these ciphers anywhere in the country. *(DB)*

This memorial plaque was on the side of St Mary's Church House, the Market Place, and commemorates its conversion from The Oxford House pub (now Adkin's estate agents). The house could be seen from the old Post Office parcel sheds. Mr Tom Tribble Tappin was the landlord of the pub from 1894 to 1907, when it was sold by Well's Brewery to Miss Hedges, who converted it into Church House. *(Don Batten)*

Chapter Nine

1981 to 2000

Remembrance Sunday, November 1987. Bob Russell in the front. To his left is Winnie Mace (née Tubb), and second person behind her is Betty Atkins, twice Mayor of Wallingford. To Mr Russell's right is Harry Nunn. On the far right of the picture is Mrs Cameron. *(DB)*

Hart Street, 1988. From 1920 to the early 1950s the sports shop was a basketmaker's owned by Henry Lavington. Before 1920 it was The King's Arms public house, and had been in existence as a public house since 1784. To the rear was where the Kilburn Press had its first premises in 1954. Hart Street is only about 300ft long but in the nineteenth century it boasted four public houses. On the corner of Wood Street and Hart Street was the Fat Ox, while at the other end of Hart Street stood The King's Arms, and between them was the Two Brewers. Opposite the Fat Ox was the Black Lion. *(DB)*

Opposite: The opening of the bridge in the Castle Grounds, 1984. The bridge was dedicated to the memory of the life and generosity of Sir John Hedges. The Mayor seen here is Pat Granados. The bridge spanned Castle Lane and allowed the public access to the Castle motte. The Castle Grounds were opened on 21 May 1978 by Viscount Harcourt, Vice Lord Lieutenant of Oxfordshire. *(JC-T)*

The Wallingford bypass: a view of the partly constructed Winterbrook Bridge, looking towards the Wallingford bank, January 1993. The construction of this bridge was delayed because Bronze Age remains were discovered on the site. *(DB)*

The Wallingford bypass, looking towards the Mongewell roundabout, January 1993. The field on the left is the Hundred Acres. Before the First World War this field was used to hold an annual military camp. Much of the area where the road runs was once covered with beech trees. *(DB)*

The opening of Winterbrook Bridge and the Wallingford bypass, 29 July 1993. Standing around the podium are Councillor John Jones, Mr D.H. Hook, the County Engineer, and representatives of Galliford Midlands, the engineers who built the bridge. When the bypass was opened the traffic in Wallingford became so light that every day seemed like a Sunday afternoon. *(AB)*

The opening of the Wallingford bypass by Councillor John Jones, Chairman of Oxfordshire County Council. He is about to cut the ribbon and declare the road open. The bridge was, unfortunately, built over a favourite bathing place for local residents, called Sandy Cove. *(AB)*

The 350th anniversary celebrations in 1997 of the 1647 Siege of Wallingford during the English Civil War. The pageant was held in the Castle Grounds. The Sealed Knot re-enactment society assisted with the battle scenes. It was felt among the crowds that there were probably more people injured at these celebrations than at the original siege! The scene here depicts an assault on Wallingford Castle by the Parliamentary (Roundhead) forces under Colonel Weldon. *(DB)*

Opposite, bottom: Another scene from the from the Siege of Wallingford celebrations, 1997. Roundhead cavalry advance on Wallingford Castle. The Governor of Wallingford Castle in 1647 was Colonel Blagge. The siege lasted for sixteen weeks. Not even the fall of Oxford, the only other Royalist stronghold in the area, persuaded Blagge to surrender. But when it became obvious that no relief could ever be expected, he did surrender the Castle, on 9 July 1647. In 1652 the Council of State decided that the Castle should be demolished and the stone sold, with any profits given to the poor. Apparently this last condition was never honoured, as the money was given to Michael Molyns as compensation for supplies he gave to the Royalists. *(DB)*

Judging by this poster in a Wallingford shop window, the ghost of Oliver Cromwell still haunts the streets of Wallingford.
The Parliamentarian forces did considerable damage to the town. St Leonard's Church was used as a stable and was later badly damaged by fire, as were many houses within the town. *(DB)*

Funeral of Diana - Princess of Wales
Saturday 6th September 1997

As the time of the procession has now changed and to
enable our staff time to show their respects

THIS SHOP WILL BE

Closed on SaturdayMorning

It will Open at
1.30pm

and Close at
5.30 pm

BAKERS OVEN WILL DONATE **10%**
OF TODAY'S TAKINGS

TO:

THE FAVOURED CHARITIES OF
THE PRINCESS OF WALES

As when President Kennedy was shot, most people can remember where they were when Princess Diana was tragically killed on 31 August 1997. On the day of her funeral all shops and businesses closed for the morning. The picture shows Carl Wood's butcher's shop in St Martin's Street on that morning. *(DB)*

One of the posters put in the town's shop windows on the morning of Princess Diana's funeral. These pictures were taken at about 9.30 a.m., when there was nobody about in the town at all and the shops were closed. Some might say that this funeral was the final, great public act of the twentieth century in the UK, a century that had seen so much death and destruction. Hopefully we can learn the lessons of that past century and allow our children and grandchildren to inherit a more peaceful future. *(DB)*

ACKNOWLEDGEMENTS

In compiling this book, I am indebted to many people for their help. First and foremost is Joyce Huntley. But for her knowledge and seemingly inexhaustible supply of photographs, the book would have been much the poorer. Margaret Gardener and Janet Anderson also deserve a special mention. James Spooner must not be forgotten for allowing me to copy some postcards from his extensive collection. Mike Coxe proved very helpful with his knowledge of Wallingford people and Wallingford Rowing Club. John Jeskins and Ken Castle also deserve my thanks for the photographs they allowed me to copy and for all the anecdotes about Wallingford people that they passed on. The following have all been very helpful, too: Wendy Beasley, Millie Brett, Tony Crabbe, Lou Crook, Betty Dorn, Connie Green, the late John Heaton, John Hobbs, Peter Hoddinott, Harold Huntley, Richard Lay, Sidney Moody, George Motyka, Derek Packman, Don Passey, Bob Russell, Linda Shoebridge, Chris Turner, Marion Volins, Anthony Wilder, the excellent Wallingford Museum, and my friends at the Civil Service Retirement Fellowship, all of whom have earned my gratitude. I must also thank Malcolm Graham and his excellent staff at the Centre of Oxfordshire Studies. I should like to thank as well Simon Fletcher of Sutton Publishing for his patience and helpful advice. Finally I must thank my wife Ann, for without her encouragement, which at times bordered on bullying, her proofreading and her support I don't think I would have finished this book. If there is anybody who feels their name is missing from the above list, I apologise for the omission.

The griffin on the roof of the Boathouse, 1988. The building went up in 1893 on the site of the old gasworks. The ground floor was used for boat-building, while the first was an art gallery managed by Claude Rowbotham, who ran art classes and organised exhibitions of local artists. The griffin was stolen in the 1990s and found, broken into several pieces, in Watery Lane, Crowmarsh; a replacement has recently been installed. *(DB)*

Picture Credits

Janet Anderson *(JA)*; Ivy Ansell *(IA)*; George Atkins *(GA)*; Roy Atkins *(RA)*; John Atwell *(JA)*; Peter Baber *(PB)*; Johnny Barcham *(JB)*; Don Batten; David Beasley *(DB)*; Jean Beasley *(JBY)*; Ann Beasley *(AB)*; Wendy Beasley *(WB)*; Boots Ltd *(BL)*; Jean Calvin-Thomas *(JC-T)*; Ken Castle *(KC)*; Centre for Oxfordshire Studies *(COS)*; Colin Clarke *(CC)*; Mike Coxe *(MC)*; Tony Crabbe *(TC)*; Lou Crook *(LC)*; T. Dearlove *(TD)*; Judy Dewey *(JD)*; Margaret Gardener *(MG)*; John Heaton *(JHN)*; Peter Hoddinott *(PH)*; Joyce Huntley *(JH)*; John Jeskins *(JJ)*; T. Jordan *(TJ)*; Mr Lamble *(ML)*; Richard Lay *(RL)*; Mrs Marchbanks *(MM)*; Sid Moody *(SM)*; Tony Morris *(TM)*; George Motyka *(GM)*; Derek Packman *(DP)*; Don Passey *(DPY)*; Catherine Rickards *(CR)*; Brian Robbins *(BR)*; Olive Robinson *(OR)*; Linda Shoebridge *(LS)*; Bill Tappin *(BT)*; Chris Turner *(CT)*; Marion Volins *(MV)*; Harold Waite *(HW)*; Wallingford Fire Brigade *(WFB)*; Wallingford Museum *(WM)*; Elizabeth Warwick *(EW)*; Anthony Wilder *(AW)*.

Meal time for Wallingford Boy Scouts at their summer camp at Basildon Park, August 1912. The third boy on the left is Alexander Macfarlane, from Howbery Park, who in December that year died tragically while being operated on in a London Hospital; he was buried at Crowmarsh Church. *(JH)*